Successfully Marketing Your Novel In The 21st Century

Written by
Austin S. Camacho

With Contributions by
Sandra Bowman

ISBN: 978-0-9893696-4-0

Published by:
Intrigue Publishing
10200 Twisted Stalk Ct
Upper Marlboro, MD 20772

Cover Design by Iconix

Printed in the United States of America
Printed on Recycled Paper

Foreword

This book is the second edition of one you may already have on your shelves, even though the title is a bit different. Authors often update how-to manuals with new material, but titles don't generally change. I think you deserve an explanation for that, but I have to take you back to bring you up to date.

I wrote my first full-length work in 1985 in the infancy of home computers. I submitted that first, admittedly awful, manuscript to publishers and agents with predictably disastrous results. I kept writing, improving with each attempt, yet the results continued to be the same. In 1999, at a time when I thought I had a manuscript that others would really enjoy reading, I learned about a new publishing option called print on demand. I couldn't afford thousands of dollars to self-publish then, but for a couple of hundred dollars I could get a book published and find out for sure if I was deluding myself about my writing. I turned my words into a book through POD publisher "Buy Books on the Web."

As it turned out, a lot of people wanted to read *Blood and Bone* and I got a lot of positive feedback. Within three years, my publisher had changed its name to Infinity Publishing. By then, there was a lot of competition in the POD marketplace, but few people had found much success because most authors didn't understand the necessity of marketing their work. I was one of Infinity's most successful writers, so the company asked me to write a guidebook for their other authors. *Successfully Marketing Print-on-Demand Fiction* hit shelves in 2003. Since then I've moved to self-publishing and publishing with a small press.

Aside from short stories published in other peoples' anthologies I have five novels in my Hannibal Jones detective series in print plus four novels in my Stark and O'Brien action thriller series. I've spoken dozens of times at writer's conferences, seminars, book clubs and civic organizations. And I've sold nearly 10,000 copies of my novels. In that time I've heard two things from readers of my marketing book. First, I was told that most marketing books for authors were filled with tips that were valuable only to nonfiction writers and that my book was the only one on the market just for fiction writers. Second, readers told me that many of the tips I offered were also valuable to those who didn't choose the POD option, that just about anyone who had not yet landed a contract with a major publisher could benefit from my marketing approach.

All of that inspired the current title of this book and an improved edition to embrace a broader audience. It was the best I could do at the time, but the publishing world has continued to change–so radically in the last ten years that cutting edge has become obsolete. New options have arisen to challenge the major publishers, such as companies who offer the POD process to self-publishing authors, the loss of a major bookstore chain and bookstore chains that offer to publish books themselves.

New avenues for selling books have appeared, from e-books to "big box" stores like Costco and Sam's Club, to online book clubs that offer samples for their subscribers to read before making a purchase. Local book clubs have become a force for driving best sellers, The Internet has changed everything we do, from writing to publishing to marketing. And authors boasting major success on the Kindle, at conferences and in independent bookstores are preaching that authors need to take more responsibility in getting their work into the hands of readers. In this third edition, I've added a lot to try to show you what I've tried since the first edition.

Now that you know the "why" of this book, let's get down to the "how" of making your novel a success.

Austin

For my lovely wife Denise, master of formatting and editing whiz, who tolerates my obsession with "the writing thing" with grace and a smile, and without whom my successes would be nowhere near as sweet.

GETTING STARTED

"The journey of a thousand miles begins with a broken fan belt and a leaky tire."

1. What This Book Is...and Isn't

Before we get started, you should know what you've bought. First, this is NOT a book about how to be a better writer. You'll find no grammar and punctuation instruction, no treatise on character development or setting, and no tips on dialogue or prose construction. This book assumes that you have already written your novel and now want people you don't know to buy it and, with any good fortune, recommend it to their friends who will also buy it.

This is NOT a book on how to get rich. I haven't met a single print-on-demand (POD), self-published or small press author yet who has gotten wealthy writing fiction. On the other hand, there are probably only a dozen people writing fiction right now in all forms of publishing who have made a fortune. You surely know their names because their novels have become movies, which is where the wealth is. Even among the big-name publishers, the novelists who make a good living on their writing alone are the exception, not the rule. Like myself, most of those people are writers because they feel they have no choice. They have stories to tell. So, if your primary reason for being a writer is to make lots of money, I strongly recommend that you quit now and save yourself a world of heartache.

This is also not a textbook on general marketing. The information herein will not help you much if you want to sell cars, jewelry, or real estate. It will be only marginally useful if you have a nonfiction book other than narrative nonfiction such as memoir. And if your book has been picked up by a mainstream publisher who gave you a six-figure advance, much of this may be irrelevant to you. That degree of focus is not a mistake.

When I published my first novel through Infinity Publishing (then called Buy Books on the Web.com) in 1999, both that company and the POD concept were in their infancy. To their credit, the folks at Infinity were very up front about the services they offered. They made it clear that it was up to me to sell my books. I will always appreciate the fact that they made no promises about marketing. They promised only to create a quality product from the manuscript I sent them, and they never let me down on that score.

Infinity is not unique in the marketing area. Most POD publishers offer two options in the marketing arena: nothing at all or a little help for a lot of money. By and large, POD companies are not large publishers moving into a new market. They are primarily printing companies offering a service to authors.

After I learned more about the business, I created my own company and published my own books. I knew from day one that selling my books was entirely up to me. I had entered a business where profit margins are paper thin and respect for a little guy on his own is even thinner.

With that experience under my belt I published with Echelon Press, which with about seventy authors on board was still considered a small press. My publisher, Karen Syed, was as honest with me as the Infinity team. Before she accepts manuscripts, she explains to authors that she expects them to spend their energy, time, and a certain amount of money on promoting their novel. Unlike the POD companies, small presses like Echelon are able to foster team spirit, inspiring their authors to collaborate and combine their marketing efforts.

On the other hand, major publishers have extensive marketing channels in place, business relationships with the major chain bookstores and a sales force dedicated to getting books onto bookstore shelves. As a group, small presses and POD publishers are learning, and someday they may find ways to do everything that Random House and Penguin do. Not that it would matter much to you. Except for their dozen or so best sellers, big-name publishers don't offer much marketing support for their authors either. So, the novelists who get that advance from Random House often get a shock that you won't. You already know that marketing is your responsibility.

My professional background in public affairs prepared me to deal with the mass media, but I knew I was not a marketing expert. POD was new when I started but self-publishing was not, and I read a number of excellent volumes on how to market self-published books. You'll find my favorites listed in Appendix A.

Still, none of those books did a good job of addressing my specific needs. The most successful self-published books are nonfiction entries. Much of the best advice on marketing nonfiction books won't help you get your novel into readers' hands. So I set about culling out what was most useful to me. A lot of trial and error was involved, and more than a few disappointments. This book is the result of the synthesis of knowledge found in those books, my public affairs training, and my hard won personal experience.

Marketing—it's not just an adventure, it's a job

Among my own marketing efforts is an e-mail newsletter that I send to just about anyone willing to accept it on a regular basis. The most common reply I get to my newsletter is generally something like "Damn, when do you sleep?"

I do spend a good deal of my free time marketing my fiction. Most weekends I'm some place signing books. That's because I've learned that people want to take away a piece of the author with them when they leave and, for me, personal appearances are fun and profitable.

Your level of success will depend largely on how much time you invest. I view my writing as my hobby and I don't think I spend more time on it than a lot of other people spend on fishing, bowling, or role-playing games.

But, you say, "I want to spend my time telling stories, not selling books." Hey, me too. But I've spoken to a number of commercially published writers and what I learned from them has changed my view of this business. Most mystery authors are expected to "drop" a novel a year. This all makes good marketing sense. Nothing drives the sales of a first book as much as the publication of a second or third novel. Publishers give these authors a set schedule that only leaves four months for writing and another four months for the editing process.

What I find most interesting is that these writers are expected to spend the same amount of time, four months out of the year, on a circuit of book signings, conference appearances, and television/radio interviews. In other words, they are expected to spend as much time marketing their books as writing them. I looked at that model and decided that if it's so popular among the big publishers, there must be something to it. I now spend roughly as much time on marketing as I do on writing. If you want to push your sales to impressive levels, I suggest you do the same. It's a lot of work, but it's also very rewarding. And I've found a lot of it to be great fun.

Select from the menu

Unless you're interested in a full-time job marketing your books, I don't expect you to do everything I suggest in this book. I am sharing a broad variety of ideas, and even I don't do all these things all the time, although I have personally tried nearly all of them. Some things worked better than others for me. Some things that didn't work were fun, so I kept doing them. Some things that worked well were so unpleasant I decided to drop them from my plan. I strongly recommend that you try everything that looks workable to you, track your results, and decide on your own what's best for you.

One man's opinion

Every word in this volume is based on my experiences and feelings. Someone out there will disagree with everything I say, and many people have the right to do so. Remember, I started this trip with the same leaky tire you may have now, but then I fixed up my marketing vehicle so that it ran pretty well and took me where I wanted to go. I used what I learned to successfully self-publish, and decided to regain the rights to the properties I had published through a small press. I encourage you to be open to the ideas of others and follow your instincts. If you come up with a great idea I didn't think of, send me an e-mail (at ascamacho@hotmail.com) so I can add it to the next edition!

2. Basic Principles

If you're reading this book, you probably already know the advantages of POD publication. It's the author-friendly space between needing some commercial publisher's editorial process to approve your book for publication and needing thousands of dollars to create your own publishing company and self-publish a few thousand copies of your book. But there are a lot of differences between POD, traditional self-publishing and being commercially published. Most of the ideas in this book are impacted by those differences.

The book matters

Surprised? I know you think you've created a piece of timeless literature, but to the person about to hand over his or her $14.95 plus tax, it's a product and it had better be high quality. You have to start with a book someone wants to read. Know your genre and write something that is not only good but also easily classified and recognizable. When one early reader wrote that my detective novel *Blood and Bone* was "Grisham meets Shaft," I knew I'd hit the target. I had a book that fit in with what mystery readers were looking for.

It's harder to get reviews for a POD or self-published book than one that is commercially published, especially if the genre isn't obvious. If the writing doesn't bowl the reviewer over, he or she won't bother to write a review at all. If it isn't a good read, your book won't convince TV or radio hosts to speak to you. When you go to press, make sure it's your best effort. Remember, your POD publisher won't judge you—that's a plus AND a minus in this case.

Camouflage

Now that you have a book that reads like popular science fiction or romance or whatever your genre is, make sure that's obvious to the casual observer. Big publishers ensure this as a matter of course, and small presses usually do pretty well too. Their experienced book designers, artists and marketing teams create the standard look and feel. But if you're self-published or a POD author, it's up to you. Don't expect your POD publisher to mention ANY of this.

Why must your book look, feel, and smell like everyone else's? Because readers decide to buy based on a large number of subconscious signals a book sends them. They've been trained by publishers to expect certain things. They've also been conditioned by those same publishers to believe that any book worth reading will be published by them. We know that's not true, of course, but a book that says "self-published" to the consumer also says "amateur." The same applies to booksellers. Your focus should be to make your book look as professional as possible, from the layout of the words inside to the cover art you choose.

Of course, you'll need to look, sound, and act like a professional writer too, but that should not be camouflage. That's what you are!

The POD Advantage

The primary advantage of POD publishing is that you can react more quickly than anyone else in the industry. Consider this: an author who wrote a great book and got it accepted by a mainstream publisher in August 2001 might have seen his book hit the stands around August 2002. If you used POD, your book could have been out since November 2001. Oh, and if his book was set mostly on the tenth floor of the World Trade Center, several thousand copies are now trash. If that was your POD book, on the other hand, you could quickly do a rewrite and change the location or the time period so that the next copy printed would be current. When people tell you (and they will) about that blatant typo on page 44, you can make the correction much more easily than in a traditionally published book.

When Stephen King tells you at that conference that he read your book and it scared HIM, you can get that comment on your front cover in a month or two. And if some artist presents a better idea for your cover, give the idea fair consideration. If it represents your book better than the current cover, it might be time to change it.

That mention of covers brings up the other primary advantage of POD publishing. You have a level of control over your book that only a Grisham or Clancy has in the commercial publishing world. One of my favorite authors is Lucia St. Clair Robson (www.luciastclairrobson.com). She has written some of the best historical novels on any shelf. However, her publisher wrapped her first book in a cover that screamed "historical romance." Lucia's work transcends the usual romance writing, to the point that a later book, *Ghost Warrior*, was one of two finalists for the Western Writers of America's Spur Award for best Western of the year. If Lucia had been self-published or a POD author, she could have made sure the cover of her first book was fitting for her work.

Control of your book as a physical entity goes well beyond the cover. Typeface, margins, the way chapter headings are set up and headers and footers are just a few of the things you could choose to dictate. Depending on the company you work with, you may even be able to decide whether or not your book is printed on recycled paper. There are dozens of choices involved.

But I do have to remind you that most of the choices publishers make about books they publish are made for some sane reason. While you're working to create a book that will make you happy, remember that you won't be paying cover price for a copy. Ultimately you want to design a book that complete strangers will want to pick up, so keep one eye on the principle of camouflage and make sure your book fits on the shelf with other books your readers will be looking for.

3. Get Organized

You wouldn't really start a long journey with a broken fan belt or leaky tire. It's just as important that you check your gear and prepare for your journey into marketing. You have to have a plan to get anywhere, and you have to keep your tools organized to be able to grab the one you need when you need it. Even experienced fishermen, who have their favorite flies in their hat, keep a tackle box, right?

I recommend that you get a three-ring binder in which to store a few important papers. You can get plastic document protectors to hold the papers you don't want to punch holes in. If the binder seems too cumbersome to you, chuck it after a while. But it's easier to start out too organized and pare down than it is to look up one day and realize you don't have or can't find something you really need.

And before you accuse me of being old-fashioned, understand that I do keep electronic copies of almost everything. However, experience has shown me that disks wear out, computers crash, and e-mails sometimes choose to delete themselves. Consider the paper copies your backup file. Besides, sometimes it's just easier to hold a couple of pieces of paper side by side to decide which you like best.

Your promotion plan

The first tab in your notebook should be your personal promotion plan. Here is where you set up your schedule of activities that will prompt people to buy your books. List all of the techniques you will have selected to try when you've reached the end of this book. This plan can be very simple, and it can change regularly, but it will evolve into your continuing road map to success. Remember, you ultimately won't be promoting a single novel or short story collection but rather creating a market for a series of publications. By the time you go to print for your second or third book, you will have refined this plan into a clear list of objectives that not only work for you, but that you are comfortable with.

This is one place a publisher might help you. The publisher may not do your marketing for you, but it will have some experience in developing marketing plans and should be willing to share that experience. If your publisher offers you a marketing plan, for goodness sakes take it and work it, and add the ideas you see here that work for you. An example is at Figure 1.

Behind the second tab of your promotion notebook will be copies of your news releases, including their release dates. Trust me; you will want to refer back to these pieces to refine each new one. If you do any sort of mass mailing or post flyers anywhere, keep copies of these as well. Once you've perfected these wheels, you won't want to reinvent them each time.

Tab three should hold a ledger into which you can record all your costs. This may prove more challenging than you expect, but you will want to know how much your hobby or business is costing you, and how much of that money you're recovering in sales. Seeing these numbers in black-and-white will also help you to gain perspective. Should printing be that big a chunk of my promotional costs? Was that direct mailing worth the money put into it? This is where all those numbers should be laid out for your inspection.

Your reviews and testimonials should be gathered at the fourth tab. These should also be dated, with contact information nearby. These people should all be added to your Christmas card list because they have shown their friendship. Nothing sells books as well as a good review, and as long as supporting you is rewarding, the people who gave you testimonials in the past will continue to support you to their friends and neighbors. In fact, they will most likely be willing to say nice things about your next book. Copy these reviews in a nice, clean form so that when Random House does come calling, you have something impressive to show them. And don't despair. In a few pages, I'll show you how to start that impressive collection of testimonials you'll soon be boasting about.

Your business correspondence comes next at tab five. Save everything you receive in the mail from your publisher, distributors, booksellers, fans, or anyone else who writes to you regarding your writing. I know you're way smarter than I am, but you still won't remember all those names and faces. Nor will you remember the details of your business dealings. This way, you don't have to.

The sixth and final tab is most important to POD authors. You must maintain a copy of every edit, change and revision your book receives after your first printing. If you've chosen the right publisher, you'll be able to get corrections made quickly and generally without much expense. (This was a major reason I chose Infinity.) Someday you'll want to send someone an excerpt from your book, and you'll want to make sure the electronic version you have hidden on a disk matches what's in your actual published product.

That's how you will build and track your plan. But how will you choose the tactics that will be in it?

Evidence-based marketing

In the years since I was asked to write a marketing guide for POD novels, I have self-published seven novels. A small press did pick up my flagship novel,

Blood and Bone which, aside from a modest advance, got me better distribution (more on this later.). I have also spent a good deal of time, money and energy, on marketing. I have learned three important things:

1. What worked for someone else may not work for me.
2. The person pushing a marketing idea may not really care whether or not it increases my sales, as long as he or she gets paid.
3. Some of the traditional wisdom may no longer apply.

The publishing landscape changes every day.

For those reasons I've come to keep very careful records and to challenge everything I do in the marketing arena. I've developed what seems to me to be a very obvious marketing concept: *evidence-based marketing*. Before I invest in a tactic, I consider the cost and project how many books it will have to move to be considered a winner. Whenever I try a new idea, I try to figure out some sort of measurement by which I can objectively judge if it was successful. And whenever someone offers to help me for a price, I ask specific questions about the success of previous clients. If a publicist or marketing expert is unwilling to offer any kind of guarantee, there is often a reason.

Most of what you see in this book has worked for me, but I've also included a few ideas that sounded good but didn't pay off. You'll see these "good ideas that didn't work" scattered through the text. Who knows? They might work for you.

Austin S. Camacho

PASSIVE MARKETING

"Hard work will pay off in the future. Laziness pays off now."

4. Build Your Book

Your passive marketing tool kit includes all the things that sell books for you when you aren't selling them yourself. You might call them automatic salesmen. They convince people to buy your book when you're not around.

If you plan to be active with passive marketing, the first step is to create a book that people will want to pick up. Note I didn't say write a book. The content may be fantastic, but it's not a marketing tool. I'm talking about creating the physical package.

If you self-publish, you will be responsible for every decision about the look and feel of your book. POD publishers generally leave a lot of the format decisions to you as well. Even small presses often look for your approval or input in creating your physical book. That means that you need to become as smart about the appearance of your book as you are about the actual writing. Commercial publishing houses have mastered the little subconscious signals that say to the consumer, "This is the one you want." How do you become as canny about book packaging as they are? Look closely at what they do.

Get out from behind your keyboard and spend some time in the appropriate section of the biggest bookstore in town. What is the common pattern of covers that says, "I'm a techno-thriller," for example? How many pages long are they? What type size and style is most common? Do they have chapter headings or just numbers? Are there headers or footers showing the title, author, or page number? How is the back cover copy set up? What does that copy say? Take notes and figure out how you'll imitate these standard techniques.

Are most of your favorite covers separate back and front creations, or are they wraparound covers, that is, one big picture that covers the front and back of the book? I noticed that the mysteries that caught my eye usually had wraparound covers, so I knew I wanted one for *Blood and Bone*. When that book went to Echelon Press, the people there followed suit, which reinforced the wisdom of my choice. And while they went for a very different look, their cover artist turned in an effort that screams "mystery/detective" as loudly as the original.

Check out author photos as well. I've found these to be very popular on POD back covers. However, they are rare on genre fiction back covers, and even on mainstream fiction you don't see them as often as you used to. There's good reason for this. The back cover copy is one of the most powerful passive marketing tools. Unless the author is a celebrity, a photo on the back is wasting prime marketing space.

Size Matters

Currently, POD publishers for the most part produce paperbacks that are 8.5 by x 5.5. This is close to but not exactly equivalent to traditional publishers' trade paperback size. Trade paperbacks are typically nine by six or 9 by 5, which makes an 8.5 by x 5.5 book scream POD. Of course, all trade paperbacks are larger than most of the paperbacks you and I buy—not that there's anything wrong with that. While you're in the bookstore, pay the most attention to how other trade paperbacks are laid out and designed. Look at hard covers as well. You might see some ideas there you really like. Consider whether or not books like yours are even published in trade paperback or mass market paperback size. And if you're looking at hardcover books, check whether books like yours have dust jackets.

Straighten Your Spine?

Generally, I agree with the tips given in other books on marketing books. Anytime my opinion is at odds with the group, I feel I should point it out. This is one such opinion.

Well-respected volumes in titles about marketing books recommend that you print the lettering on your book's spine so that it will be right side up when the book is standing on a shelf. There is some sound thinking behind this idea. As a reader approaches a shelf lined with books, he will be able to read your title without tipping his head to the side. That could mean he reads yours first, and that could make all the difference.

However, I believe the camouflage principle takes precedence. When you conduct your bookstore visual survey, check the orientation of the spines on the books in your genre. If they vary, then being upright could be all right. But if they're all turned on their side, and especially if they're all facing the same way, it would be wiser to conform, thus reinforcing that your novel is a member of the group in good standing. If all the other books on the shelf have their spines written sideways, readers scanning the shelf will hurt their necks to read yours or just pass it by.

Cover Story

Once you know what you want in a book cover, you have to decide on its source. Small presses have artists all lined up. Most POD publishers will create a cover for you, usually at no extra cost. While this is a very personal decision, my view is that every artist has a personal style and POD publishers don't have too many artists on staff. Therefore, the covers from any given publisher will have a certain feel of similarity.

When it came time to create a cover for my first novel in print, *Blood and Bone*, I got a good recommendation from Infinity's author advocate, John Harnish. He pointed me to Cat Wong, a commercial artist on the other side of the country. Cat was willing to do a couple of things that were important to me, starting with reading my book. Having seen my style and the story, she came up with an excellent cover concept. She was also willing to send several reworks until I was completely satisfied with the final result.

Of course, if you hire an artist yourself, the money comes out of your own pocket. But I can't count the number of people who have told me that the cover made them pick up my book and look inside, and once they did, they were much more likely to take a copy home. I know my cover drove sales, so I figured it was money well spent.

Don't know where you can find a good artist who's willing to take the time to get to know your work? I searched online and found a large number of commercial artists willing and able to give me what I needed. I interviewed several of them by email and finally settled on Iconix (iconix.biz) who gave me very professional work in the $150 to $300 range.

If I had to do it all again I might try a more local resource. I would call the nearest art college. Many of the students are incredibly talented, and their first or second paying job will be very important to them. They're willing to listen, want the exposure, and want you to be satisfied. There's a bonus for them in that they might be able to get course credit for designing your cover. The bonus for you is that they may not charge you much for the chance to get their art on a book cover. In fact, some excellent artists may do the work for a byline in the book and a couple of signed copies.

I must point out that other respected people in the industry will disagree with this advice. After all, a cover is not a work of art, but the most important promotional vehicle your book has. Someone who has never designed a book cover may not speak the language or understand the subconscious signals we talked about earlier. If you do choose to seek out a student as your cover artist, be sure to give him or her copies or photos of successful, recently published books in your genre as a starting point. The less experience your artist has, the more your judgment will matter, but you can both get off to a better start if you point out a few covers on Amazon.com or BN.com that feel right to you.

When you think you've got the cover you want, give it the acid test at your favorite bookstore. Take a picture of your cover to the manager and ask for a reaction. If she says, "Nice artwork! What's the book about?" then you haven't reached your perfect cover yet. On the other hand, if she says, "Cool? A new political thriller?" then you know your cover's a winner.

The Price of Success

One way POD books often stand out from their commercial peers is the cover price. This is a very important point for both you and bookstore managers. I'm an unknown mystery author. If my book is out of line with Grisham's on a "pennies per page" basis, it will be snubbed.

Often, POD publishers don't give you much latitude concerning the price of your book. For example, when I published with Infinity, a book that was 200 pages long could not sell for less than $13.95. If the book was 201 pages, the minimum cover price was $14.95. Most POD publishers still price by page count, and in most cases their cover prices are higher than equivalent books from mainstream publishers.

There are things you can do to bring the price down to the level of other books on the shelf, assuming your company gives you as much control over formatting as Infinity does. First, take a look at the margins, the amount of white space around the edge of your pages. If it can be reduced without making your book too different from your competitors, ask the publisher to do so. Second, look closely at the white space on chapter head pages. Compare kerning (space between letters) and leading (space between lines) in your book to others on the shelf. Can you push lines together to save a few pages?

However, don't sacrifice your camouflage for page count. Follow conventional book design format as much as possible. After all, you want your book to look as professional as anything else on the shelves. For example, most readers expect to see a flyleaf—a totally blank sheet—at the beginning of the book as well as a couple of pages that contain only the title and author's name. The first page of a book's text always starts on the right, almost always opposite a blank page. If your genre usually includes a page with an author's bio, don't sacrifice that either. Hang onto the font size and type that is most common in your genre. You will rarely see a book in the stores printed in Times New Roman. That is for computer keyboards and obvious POD volumes.

Polish the Insides

The camouflage principle applies just as strongly to the inside of your book as to the outside. That's one reason you want to see a sample book from your publisher or printer before you commit. Does it use the same quality paper that commercial publishers use? Cheap paper is one sign of an amateur printing press.

Just as you rely on an outside professional to design your cover if you are self-publishing or using a POD company, hire a professional editor and proofreader whenever it's within your budget. The objective is to make the book look professional! Typographical mistakes and misspellings don't cut it in the big leagues. You say you saw typos in the last Nelson DeMille you read? Maybe, but he doesn't have anything to prove, and neither does his publisher. You do, so make your book perfect.

When your reviews start pouring in, go back to the bookstore to see how they're used in your genre. In my case, a few reviews are often posted on the first inside page. So, guess what I've done with the first few reviews of *Collateral Damage?* That's right.

5. Join the Club

As soon as you start calling yourself a carpenter, you are expected to join the local union. If' you're an author, you should belong to your local writers' group. These groups are everywhere and generally easy to find by doing an Internet search of "writers club" and your city's name or watching the community bulletin board in your local newspaper or at the library. Groups in my area include the Writer's Center in Bethesda, Maryland; the Maryland Writers Association; and the Virginia Writers Club. I belong to all three.

You say you're not the social type? Yeah, that's what they all say. Writing is a lonely business, beloved by introverts because communicating in writing is easier than doing it face to face. But you'll be surprised at the friendships and fun you will find when you actually join one (or three) of the local groups in your area. These are people who are just like you.

There are a lot of good reasons to join a writers' group, but here we'll only deal with those that relate to marketing. First, you want to be recognized as a writer. One way to accomplish that is to be seen with writers. Another is to be called a fellow author by published authors in your group. You can create a situation that prompts people to include your name when they talk about local authors. This very passive approach pays long-term dividends.

Networking is another valuable benefit. Chat with other writers long enough and you get to know what you need to know for your active marketing programs, such as which local book clubs like to have authors come in to speak to them and which bookstores will treat you with respect if you ask to hold a signing there. You also might meet someone who writes in your genre and would be happy to hold a joint signing.

Be Active in the Group for Passive Marketing

If you help make the arrangements for a writers' association event, book sales may find you. Such organizations often have a presence at local book fairs and other events where members can offer their books for sale without paying for space. Helping to make the contacts for such events can make it easier to get a chance to do a reading at these events or to become part of a panel of experts speaking at one. After a good panel, people may seek you out for an autographed copy of your latest book.

Writer's groups also host their own events, usually every year but sometimes more frequently. I was the conference coordinator for the Maryland Writers Association's 2003 conference. The event was quite successful, which boosted my own credibility and expanded my network. I got to know several of the speakers I booked, some of whom are leading figures in the publishing and writing world. In conjunction with that effort I promoted the conference on a local public service television station. Not only did the whole area see my face being associated with writers, but also the host of the five-minute daily program mentioned the titles of my novels on the air (priceless!) The Maryland conference always features a bookstore selling only members' and speakers' books. Quite a few of mine sold that day.

6. Get Published

Most book-marketing guides spend quite a bit of time talking about targeting your market. This is fairly easy for a book on fishing. For a sword and sorcery fantasy novel, not so much. But there is one surefire way to get the attention of those who read the kind of thing you write: appear in the magazines they read.

What to Write

If you're a novelist, you've spent some time getting to know some interesting characters. At least, they had better be interesting—you created them. Now consider: you certainly haven't packed their entire lives into your novel. So focus on a smaller part of their life, maybe something that happens right after that novel, or perhaps just before. Now write a nice short story. Give it all the attention you gave your novel and polish it just as well. This could be your first calling card that will let people know you're really a writer.

If you've had other ideas for short stories, go ahead and write them up, but don't neglect the cast of your novel. Anyone who reads the short story will already be interested in those people. They'll want to know more. I consider my Hannibal Jones short stories to be the easiest entry point for my mystery series. It will work just as well for a western, science fiction, or fantasy novel. In some genres—horror, for example— it may not be appropriate for your main characters to appear in a short story as well, but the principle still works with a different cast. If you scare me in four thousand words, I'll be eager to let you terrify me with eighty thousand.

Where to Send It

The preferred home for your short stories is inside a magazine. This time, the bookstore is not the best place to do your research. Many specialized magazines don't find a home on the local newsstand shelves. The best places to look are your local library and the Internet.

You will find a small number of magazines that carry fiction, and a few of those will be in your genre. For example, if you're a mystery writer, your search will bring up three or four small magazines, but the kings are *Ellery Queen Mystery Magazine* and *Alfred Hitchcock's Mystery Magazine*. Their science fiction counterparts are *Isaac Asimov's Science Fiction* and *Analog Science Fiction and Science Fact*. Study their submission rules, make sure your story's length is appropriate, and send it in with a good cover letter.

Figure 2 features an example of a short story cover letter.

When you've introduced yourself to all the magazines handling your genre, return to the library and ask the nice lady at the research desk for a listing of local magazines. *Down East Magazine* may not usually print romance stories, but it might print yours if you're from Maine and your story is set in Kennebunkport. Small local magazines may be easier to break into. Even if the readership is small, they're all your neighbors. That means they're the people who might show up at your next signing event.

Don't forget your fraternity or any associations to which you belong. Your alumni association magazine is always hungry for good writing, as is every club or civic organization big enough to produce its own regular publication. . Help them out while helping yourself.

Now, what do you do while you're waiting for the response from your favorite magazine? Do an Internet search for related Web sites. Mysterynet.com is one of many that posts short mysteries. The people who read them are just the folks I want to find my books. Web sites often don't pay for content, but the exposure to your targeted market can be very valuable as you build your fan base. In the same vein, look for e-zines. Again you will probably be giving away your story, but the exposure will help establish your name.

By the way, remember that writers' group you joined? Does it produce a magazine? I'll bet that publication will take your short story, and the editors will be grateful for something to fill the space.

What Else to Write

As you've surely noticed by now, some of those magazines and Web sites you checked don't take fiction at all. Now what? Well, write an article. Nonfiction writing can help you promote your books.

Wait a minute, you cry. I'm a fiction writer, remember? Sure, but you're probably a reader as well. In fact, you probably started writing science fiction after you read so much of it that you started to get disappointed in what some published authors were doing. So use that expertise. Well-written, relevant articles can net you quite a bit of activity on your website or Facebook page. You can write about anything you know about, including how to write your genre. *The Magazine of Fantasy & Science Fiction* might love to see your article on the ten best robot stories ever. If not, maybe Scifi.com would publish your essay on the sociological implications of Stargate SG1. Or, you could warm up with a piece in your writer's association newsletter on "How I Write Sci-Fi." Each time your name appears, the publication should mention your full-length work and how to order a copy. This kind of exposure can help to establish your name, your brand, with people who might not normally encounter you.

Articles should be 500 to 2,000 words in length. In addition to the markets listed about you can send them to a number of popular web sites: articlecity.com, goarticles.com, submityourarticles.com, ezinearticles.com and many others. Don't forget to add your URL in your byline. Readers who like your article will click through to check out your other work.

You are also probably qualified to write reviews. Not only will this get your name in front of readers, but can help you make connections with other authors. Like articles, reviews are a good way to get exposure and position yourself as an expert. While you can review any hot new product, I think it's most effective to review books in your own genre. Your natural interest likely has made you aware of all the latest work in your genre, and working on your own writing has made you aware of what makes a good novel in your genre. Reviews are a relatively easy way to break in to special interest magazines. Your best bet is to review a book you enjoyed. Positive reviews are more likely to see print. Express your opinion honestly, and back it up with examples from the book.

If you can review hot new books in your market, head on over to Amazon.com. In order to do this effectively you'll want to create an Amazon profile so all reviews track back to you. Be sure to sign each review with a reference to your URL (your website). You can also go to epinions.com and revoo.com to review products or books.

And offer your services to regular book review outlets. I review for International Thriller Writers, Inc. Not only have I gotten the exposure I wanted but I've done some valuable networking.

Future Use

I shouldn't even have to say this, but just in case: Don't throw those short stories and articles away. You'll be able to wrap them together in the future as an anthology or compilation that will be a fine companion to your novels. Make sure when you sell those short pieces you only surrender first-use rights or one-time use rights so you can reuse them forever.

And speaking of anthologies—if you've managed to get a novel placed with a small press put a bug in the publisher's ear. The publisher of Echelon Press was moved by the impact the 2007 wildfires had on Southern California. Rather than just sit around feeling bad, she contacted twenty of her authors for submissions and published an anthology to benefit the fire victims. Everyone involved donated our profits or royalties to the cause, but the good will and exposure was priceless. My name was associated with a timely cause, and my fictional private detective Hannibal Jones found a new audience with the publisher and twenty other authors promoting the anthology.

7. Build Your Web Site

If you don't have an Internet presence, no one will take you seriously. A great web site can be a fantastic marketing tool. First, people can learn all about you and your writing at their own pace, in their own good time. Second, the Internet is one environment in which no one knows if you're a one-person operation or a huge corporation. It all looks the same through the monitor screen. Finally, your Web site can be a point of sale, making sales for you even while you sleep. That's why they call it passive marketing.

For many writers, this will be the center of their marketing efforts. Your web site is your home port and your identity. You can do it yourself, but I believe this is one of the places it makes sense to hire an expert. Just keep an eye on them to make sure they follow a few simple guidelines.

Master of Your Own Domain

It's pretty easy these days to find someone who will build a Web site for you for a small fee. A friend might do it for a thank-you and a six-pack. And if you are old enough to have Web-savvy kids, ask them to make you one like the one they built for themselves.

Of course, if you know how to write in HTML or have the patience to learn, you can build your Web site yourself. My lovely wife, Denise, bought a copy of *HTML for Dummies* and knew enough to get started after one weekend. Even without HTML knowledge, web sites like Webs.com offer fine templates you can use to build a nice online home for your books. A fine example is B. Swangin Webster's author site (bswanginwebster.webs.com/) built on that platform.

There are plenty of places to build a free Web site. That's not where you ultimately want to be, but it's a great place to build a practice site. Angelfire, GeoCities, and Tripod all have great tutorials that walk you through the basics. You can set up a site for free and get a feel for what looks good and where the links go.

When it's time to build your real site, you'll want to find a host and buy a domain name. The name will be exclusive to you, and you should make it something easy to remember that ties in to your name, your book titles, or a continuing character. One problem with the free sites is that you can't keep your URL simple or short. For example, my first free Web site was www.angelfire.com/ dc/bloodandbone.

Today's www.ascamacho.com is a lot easier for people to keep in their heads.

Web hosting costs money, but unless you're building the megasite from hell, it's pretty easy on the wallet. I have used HostSave, which ran me about twenty-five dollars per quarter and gives me more space than I ever used. For a little more, you could buy additional URLs that went to the same place. In my case my URL was based on my name, but if you think character and type in www.hannibaljonesmysteries.com you still went to my site.

I eventually shifted the site to GoDaddy, which is a little more robust, and I kept the same URLs.

What Goes on Your Web Site

The first key to a good web site is to keep it simple. Don't try to put everything you want readers to know on the front page. Layer the information, so that the deeper visitors dig the more details they get.

You needn't agonize over a fancy name. Stephen King's official web site is titled "StephenKing.com— The Official Web Site." What you do need is to list all the reasons to buy your book. Press releases should be posted there as well as your book covers and a synopsis of your novels. Every review and testimonial you get should be on the site as well. Sample chapters are good too. Don't be afraid of giving too much away. People have been known to post entire books for download on their sites, and still sell a bunch of them.

Don't forget that people want to know about you, not just your writing, so include a good bio at the site. A calendar of events will keep visitors updated on places they can meet you in person. Pictures help them connect with you, especially if they are pictures of you at book events.

You should also make contacting you through your web site easy. Readers love to make contact with writers, so place a link on the front of your web site that sends an email to your inbox. Any feedback about your work, your site or your last appearance is a chance to turn a reader into a fan.

You might also want to add a guest book so fans can sign in, and sign up to receive your newsletter. All this mechanical stuff is freeware you can download with ease from places like Lycos (htmlgear.tripod.com), if it isn't already built into the software you are using to build your website.

Get Creative

Your site must be both fun and useful. To encourage repeat visitors it is best to have some content that is not directly oriented to selling your books. This value-added content makes visitors feel they gained something from being on your site.

This is your chance to be creative. For example, my first novel, *Blood and Bone*, revolves around a teenager dying of leukemia and my main character, Hannibal Jones, who must find the boy's missing father for a last-chance bone marrow transplant. My site, www.ascamacho.com, holds essays on bone marrow transplantation for those who might want to know more as well as more in-depth contact information on the subject. I've also added essays on hard-boiled fiction and short features about my favorite authors.

To help people get to know you, you could get a journalist friend to interview you and post the interview on your site. It might be even more fun to have your friend interview the hero or heroine of your novel. Want to go further? How about an interview with the villain?

Include some freebies such as the short stories you've written (you did write some, didn't you?) and samples of future books. In my case, Hannibal's girlfriend, Cindy, is a great Cuban cook, so my site has her favorite recipes.

Contests are a great way to make your site fun and build traffic. How about a writing challenge? You write the opening of a book and invite visitors to add the next chapter. This could evolve into a contest with some simple prize for the best submission.

Open up your imagination. One advantage of a Web site over a book is that you can change any part of it at any time, so if you don't like what you put up there, take it down. In fact, the more often you change your site, the more likely people are to come by again and again.

What People Like

Several years of web surfing have taught me a few things that turn me off when I get to a Web site, and I don't want any of those things on my own site. The most important key here is to remember that not everyone has a state of the art computer or a high speed fiber optic line running to it.

For those reasons, keep the animation and sound to a minimum. Those things take forever to load, and in that time a visitor could change his mind and move on to another site.

Those of us with less than panoramic monitors find frames a pain in the butt. Use buttons to get to other pages, but leave the frames out.

And when I get to your site, don't make me scroll down a mile long page. It's annoying as heck. Besides, the more pages you have the better. I like hopping from page to page. Make sure I can read what you write. If the print is too small, the colors too bright, or the background too distracting, I'll move on.

The Order Page

Now we've had our fun, we've seen what's useful to us, and we've made it to the heart of your site.

If you are working with a POD company, there's more money to be made by buying books and selling them than through sales in bookstores or the company's site, so you may want to get those direct sales. If you are self-publishing, an order page is essential. Either way, if you personally handle fulfillment you can promise autographed books. Now that the reader is suitably impressed, you could simply ask him to mail you a check, but there's a better way. Get set up to accept credit cards.

There is more than one way to skin that particular feline, but my favorite is the one that's free. You can download everything you need from www.Paypal.com and today almost everyone is used to using their service. PayPal takes the credit card order and deposits the cash in your account the same day, minus a 2 percent charge. For most paperbacks that will be about thirty cents per book, which leaves a good deal more money than I get when someone orders a book from Amazon.com, for instance. And when you're taking orders, don't chase business away with exaggerated postage charges. Media mail is pretty cheap, so get just enough to cover it.

I started out that way but today, if you go to www.ascamacho.com/order/ordering.html, you'll see click-through buttons to Amazon.com. I made the change because I reached the point where it was taking too much of my time to fill orders. I established an Amazon Advantage account, which gives me a little more money every time someone orders through my site. You can play around with the ordering buttons a bit to see how the system works. And if you accidentally order one of my novels, well, let me know how you enjoyed your copy.

Whatever system you choose, make sure it is easy to purchase your books. Put the "purchase" button in obvious places. The more clicks a reader has to make to get your book in his hand the less likely he is to end up with it.

If You Build It, Will They Come?

If your Web site is fun, interesting, and useful, people will want to surf to it. But you might want to help them find you. The most obvious way is to make sure you're listed on the major search engines. That way, when I Google you, I won't have to search through twelve pages of links to find you.

A sneakier way is to add lots of metatags. That's computer language for words on your opening page that readers don't see. Search engines see these hidden words. For example, a search for "giants of hard-boiled fiction" brings you to an essay by that title on my site. Hannibal Jones's girlfriend, Cindy, has her own page and since cooking is one of her hobbies, "Cuban recipes" will tickle your search engine as well. Each time you add a keyword search engines will see, you're adding more avenues for people to find you.

Another good way to increase traffic is with your related links page. If you list your favorite sites, preferably those related to your books, you could exchange links with others. People surfing their sites will be able to hop to yours with the touch of a button.

You will also want to join a Web ring or two. The "All About Romance Web Ring" links related sites like a string of Christmas tree lights. A reader on one site hits the button and is magically transported to another romance writer's site. Everyone who comes to your site through a Web ring is already interested in your type of book at least.

Remember that list of magazines you compiled back in Chapter 6? Send an announcement to each of them for their "What's new" sections. Your new site is news, especially to folks who want to read the kind of books you write.

8. Working the Web

Don't think that you're through with the Internet just because your Web site is in place. If you have the time and interest, you and the Internet can become close friends, and that friendship can generate untold book sales.

The New World of Cyber Selling

When I embarked on this marketing journey and wrote my first marketing manual (way back in 2003), everyone seemed to already know that you needed a site. But time has passed and like home computers themselves, having an online presence has become both more important and more user-friendly. These days, being seen on just one URL is simply not enough. When someone Googles you, you want a long list of links to appear. I've increased my Internet visibility in a number of ways, most of them free.

You've probably heard a lot of talk about marketing on the internet – maybe to the point that you think it's the only thing that matters. While I won't agree with that, I will say that if you want to sell e-books it makes good sense to look for your readers where they already are. E-book readers are more likely to be on line than reading ads in a printed newspaper.

People hanging out on line are most likely involved in social media sites. But how can social networks help your writing business? Well, that's largely about establishing your brand and distinguishing you from the rest of the universe. To sell you want to be a recognizable name. You want to have an internet presence so if someone Googles you they get more hits than they know what to do with.

Embarking on an Internet marketing campaign doesn't have to be difficult, tricky, or complicated. Here are a few ideas you can easily implement to get tons of traffic to your web site or your book's page on Amazon.com right now!

Blog is the Word

Blog is a contracted form of the phrase "Web log," and the first few I saw were just that, sort of a daily diary that people kept online. Now, they've become more specialized. If your book lends itself to an extended conversation about a particular subject, a blog is a good way to draw interested readers into your world. Just post a comment daily if you have time or even weekly or a couple times a month. Understand that the more often you post, the more people are likely to view your words. And the more people go to your blog, the more people are likely to get interested in your book.

Blog entries should be fairly short. I'd say four hundred words is enough, and twelve hundred words is probably too much. If your books are set in a particular area, localize your blog. A blog is a chance to chat with your fans on a regular basis. Pick a subject or theme that interests you and may be of interest to your readers. My blog is about the writing life, a subject that has attracted lots of guest bloggers.

But your blog doesn't have to be about your writing. Do you have a hobby? One of my favorite blogs is B. Swangin Webster's entitled "BSW-- Books, Shoes, Writing." She says it was created "because I love three things the most: Books, Shoes and Writing, not necessarily in that order." She keeps it interesting for readers, writers AND lovers of fine stilettos. www.booksshoeswriting.blogspot.com

If you're a fiction writer, you may need to stretch your imagination to find a suitable subject for your blog. It helps to have an opinion about something. Opinions spark responses, and comments draw other comments. A lot of blogs are politically or socially oriented; if you have a cause you want to support, a blog is a good place to voice that support. Just try to be interesting, and make it clear that you invite comments from readers.

Barry Eisler writes a series about a contract killer named John Rain who once worked for the CIA. It was easy for him to find a subject people would want to talk about, and any conversation about the political impact of CIA activity leads directly to his novels.

Does your fictional protagonist have a special interest? If she knits you could write a blog about knitting. This would not only attract a certain group of readers, but let them know they have something in common with your protagonist.

If you write a series character, you might want to try my approach. I had Hannibal Jones start a blog. I wrote each entry in the first person, as if Hannibal himself were talking to readers. In this way I was able to deepen his character and that of his supporting cast. I hope that people who read the blog get to know my detective better and want to read his adventures, although I don't have any hard evidence of this, those few who have left comments have said they would check out my novels. An unintended consequence of writing this blog is that I got to know my characters better. It was also a good place for me to practice writing short stories.

Whatever you decide to write about, you need to post at LEAST once a week. Twice a week is better, and every day is better still…but who has the time to do that? And, time aside, when you've been writing a blog for a while, you may discover that you just don't have all that much to say. If it were easy to be cute or insightful or even informative every day, more blogs would last beyond the first couple of months. Instead, most start strong, but then see ever widening gaps between entries. Luckily, as a member of a writing community you have a good option open to you.

There is a way to have a blog that has fresh content every day without draining your brain cells. Consider joining, or starting, a team blog. Take a look at what they're doing at The Kill Zone (killzoneauthors.blogspot.com).

This blog presents the musings of 11 top thriller and mystery authors. Each has a fan base, and the blog promotes cross pollination between those groups. This is how you can write one blog entry per week (or in this case, one each 11 days) be exposed to a lot of potential future fans. Just fill your group out with authors whose fans will like your work too.

This idea of several authors each submitting a little essay once a week or so is popular, and the result is a blog with daily postings. Check out Word Flirts (www.wordflirts.blogspot.com) or the Acme Authors Blog (acmeauthorslink.blogspot.com) to see how this can work very nicely. That last one features several of my pals, including Norm Cowie, Todd and Terri Stone, Rob Walker, and Morgan Mandel, who established the Book Place network. However, I must admit that my personal favorite team blog is Murderati (www.murderati.typepad.com) where my friend Ken Bruen and six other marvelous writers bare their souls.

Once you have a blog, one of the best ways to get people to it is to be a good blog neighbor. Comment on other people's blogs. That way you help them out and gain the attention of their readers. Don't forget to add your blog's URL to your signature.

Show Your Face in the Place

When I wrote the first version of this volume, MySpace was THE social networking Web site. It offered an interactive, user-submitted network of friends, personal profiles, blogs, groups, photos, music, and videos internationally. Today MySpace is almost unknown, and Facebook is the place to be. For an author, it's really a free second Web site. It is the dominant on line meeting place, but the way technology moves, I can only hope it still is when you read this. For now, the beauty of Facebook is that it can work as both a passive and active marketing tool.

Facebook provides a basic page template that can work as a perfect billboard to make people more familiar with you and your work. It is designed for letting people get to know you, but don't feel obligated to fill in the blanks. For example, you can easily upload your photo but many authors I know put their book cover where one would expect a face. You can use the "About Me" space to list my other URLs. You can list favorite books that are similar to your own work. That way, if someone searches for, say, James Patterson, they may stumble on my page.

In my opinion, Facebook is the most effective internet marketing took available today. The people you connect to here are called "friends" and when you build your network of friends (At this writing I have 4,230) each of them is potentially your marketing partner. Five thousand is the limit on friends, but hitting that ceiling is not a bad problem to have.

But how do you get a lot of friends? Well, I've come up with a couple of strategies that turned out to be very successful for me. First I found my actual friends and "friended" them. Then I went to each of their pages and sent each of their friends a friend request. Generally I added a note, like "Since we are both friends of X we should be friends with each other." Rarely has anyone turned me down with that approach.

There are also lots of writing related groups on Facebook you can join. In addition to state author and writer groups, each writing club and many book clubs have Facebook groups. I belong to about 2 dozen all told, including groups like The Literati, All About Books and the Black Faithful Sisters and Brothers Book club. Once you join these groups you can post your book related news to hit hundreds of readers. It's even more valuable to get into conversation with the people who read and post to these groups. Many of them are opinion leaders who will draw others to you as an author. And once people recognize your name in these groups, you can send all the members friend requests with a high success rate.

When you have a book signing set, you're attending conference or some other book-related date looms, you can create an event on Facebook and invite all your friends. It is probably the easiest way to directly notify people of your writing events, and Facebook lets you sort your friends into groups so you only invite those people who might be interested.

To confirm your identity as an author you'll also want to establish a fan page. There is plenty of space on your fan page for a video trailer, tons of photos, or any other media you'd like to share.

The people who connect to this page don't "friend" you, they "like" you. You can decide whether or not others post to your fan page (I say yes) and easily access statistics that tell you which posts are most popular and get shared. These pages have some limitations – It's difficult to invite all your friends to events, and clumsy to invite people to "like" you directly. But this is the page on which no one will expect to see personal info, and unlike your personal Facebook page, there is no limit to the number of people who can "like" you.

I recruit people to "like" me indirectly. Whenever someone accepts my friend request or sends me a friend request on my personal page I post on their page. It's usually something like, "Hello, George. Thank you for being my Facebook friend. Please also like me on my fan page. (www.facebook.com/austin.camacho.author)." That has gotten me to 988 likes so far – nearly a quarter of the number of friends on my personal page.

On Facebook, even your friend list can be a selling point. Nearly every author you've ever heard of has a Facebook page at this point. Message them and ask to be a friend. When people visit your site, they'll see either the faces or book covers of these other big-name writers staring at them and figure you must be cool to hang with that crowd. Harlan Corben is my friend, as are Jon Land, John Gilstrap, Hank Philippi Ryan and Shemar Moore, the actor I want to play Hannibal Jones in the movies.

All of that can be set up fairly quickly and maintained in a few minutes every week. To be effective on Facebook you really do need to post SOMETHING almost every day, and post on the groups you belong to frequently. Even though you want to post something every day, do not make it about you or your books every single day. Also, do not post the same thing on forty different pages. All it does is clog up your timeline. Every time you post, a notification is sent to everyone who is your 'friend'. Imagine seeing the same name, forty times, for the same thing. It will cause people to look at your posts as insignificant. You don't want that. Instead, post sparingly and make sure you alter the times of day that you post. That is the biggest Facebook kiss of death. Don't become 'routine'. You also need to comment on other peoples' posts so that you are in and part of the conversation when you're NOT pushing your books.

Facebook is just the most popular of a number of social networking sites. You can develop a similar presence on Gather, Crimespace, and a couple others. New kids pop up all the time like Pinterest, but I have narrowed my active efforts to just Facebook and two other social media options which I'll get into now. Here is a quick little piece about Pinterest. This is not an interactive medium. This social media outlet is about 'pinning' or posting pictures. It is a big collage of all of your favorite things. In order to make this work for you, you will need to post pictures of your books, and other books that you may be featured in. You will also want to post pictures of you at your different events; like book signings or conferences. You will also then need to 'follow' people. Pinterest is just like Facebook in that regard. If you 'follow' someone they will automatically 'follow' you back and 're-pin' or repost whatever you have added to your boards. If you decide to use Pinterest you don't need to monitor or maintain it every day. A weekly check or update is all that this medium requires.

Using LinkedIn Like a Pro

Fellow author Sandra Bowman, Marketing Director for Intrigue Publishing, contributed this section on LinkedIn, the new social network for the professional.

Unlike Facebook, LinkedIn is mainly to connect with people that do what you do. You connect with them through "connections" and then you see who shares your interests. You should connect with people that you can network with either because you are both authors or based on your professional connection with them.

The first rule of LinkedIn is that you must have a profile picture. Unlike Facebook, having a cutesy picture or your book cover is not what you want on your profile; you want people to see your true person. You also want to use your real name. Look at LinkedIn as a resume. For many people that is literally true.

The next thing you want to do is complete the profile with all of your jobs and all of your skills and qualifications. You will also want to give yourself a title. For instance, if you are a speaker, put that. If you blog, make sure you include that. If you help other authors in marketing; give yourself the title of author mentor. In short, whatever you do should be listed there.

Be sure to include your websites, all of them. List your Facebook page and your twitter name and anyplace else you appear on line. And don't forget to include the links. There is nothing worse than clicking what looks like a hot link and finding out that the link is not there or that it doesn't exist.

LinkedIn is not the type of tool that works if you sit back and do nothing. You must be active with it. To make really effective use of this one, it's a good idea to log into your account every day, and join a variety of groups.

Groups are on LinkedIn in every area of life. Join as many of those groups as you can. You want to be active, not passive. Start a discussion in one of the groups. The goal here is not to sell your books but to market yourself as an author. Selling your books will be the bonus. Once you start a discussion you can move into messaging other people in your network. But don't confuse LinkedIn with Facebook or a Yahoo Group. You do not want to overload the boards with a lot of conversation. However, you can start the same conversation in different groups.

I'm not saying that you can't sell your books on LinkedIn. You can, but you have to read the 'board' rules. Just like Facebook groups, LinkedIn chat groups have moderators and some of them establish rules so as not to get 'spammed'. You can post about your books or your events under the promotion tab. Anything that goes in the main board is meant to be a discussion and you must only discuss on those boards. You can generally discuss your characters or your novels, but remember; don't offend the people on the board because the rules are there for a reason. If you are looking for places to market your book, LinkedIn is one of the new ways to do it but it takes time.

You must 'work' the boards just like you would Facebook. Only posting information about your books is a sure way to cause people to disregard anything and everything you have to say. You've got to be interactive. Join discussions and be a part of a growing community that networks for the sole purpose of learning more about the people in the same line of work.

Twitter, where less is more.

At this moment Twitter is the most popular social media engine. From a marketing standpoint, Twitter is priceless because it is so easy for people to share news. Interesting tweets get re-tweeted and each person's connections spread your network. But it has its limits: you only get 140 characters to tell your story.

So you opened a twitter account and you ask yourself, 'what do I do next?" Well the first thing you do is send out a 'tweet.' A tweet is a line of 140 characters or less that tell people about you in one or two sentences. For instance; "Hello to everyone, my name is Austin Camacho and I am an author of several novels. A detective series and a thriller series. My books are available on amazon or wherever books are sold." The three preceding sentences total 179 characters. Too long for a tweet, so you must be creative. This is how it might read: "Hello all, I am Austin Camacho, author of 7 novels-A detective series & a thriller series. My books are available on amazon & all bookstores." That fits and says all the same things. I could have just as easily said, "Hello, my name is Austin Camacho. Author of several novels. A detective & thriller series." This is much shorter, 75 characters and there is room for my website, www.ascamacho.com. Now, whenever you include a link of any kind, twitter will re-format it for you so it doesn't take up much space. And considering the number of characters at your command, almost every tweet should include a link, pointing people to more complete content on your blog, web site or Facebook page, or to the page were they can order your book online.

The next thing you want to do is start following people. But do not make the mistake that a lot of authors make. Don't follow every author that you come across. Yes, you have a lot in common but they're not likely to buy your book. You want to follow people that are a good fit with your genre of book, or your characters. If you write about news reporters, follow news people. If you write about weather girls...follow your local weather forecasters. If you write about librarians, follow librarians. Then you will want to tweet about things that pertain to them.

Author, B. Swangin Webster has followed her local traffic reporter. The first thing she did was say hello, which got an immediate response. The reporter asked about her unique name in a tweet and in response B. Swangin said, "if u say my name on yur next update, I'll tell u." Of course the woman did and so began a long string of tweets between B. and the local traffic reporter. Now every morning B. says hello and there is always a response. B. has now got a nice twitter conversation going and is garnering support for the upcoming conference that she is helping to put together.

Another way to tweet, is to re-tweet what someone else has said that you like or agree with. By re-tweeting, you gain those followers to your page as well, and that is always a good thing. It is sure to get a conversation going. Again, remember only 140 characters, including spaces so you have to be very creative in your tweets.

And remember, whenever you get a new follower, you will want to 'tweet thank them.' In others words, acknowledge them and then follow them back. A good tweeter is someone who builds up an audience and interacts with their 'followers.

When setting up your twitter account, be sure to put your face as your profile picture. The next thing you want is a short burst of words describing yourself. For instance, B. Swangin has, "Author, lover of shoes, writer and Nina to five grandchildren." She kept it short, to the point and all about her. You should never overload your audience.

Then you will want to choose your background. B. Swangin has the cover of her second novel as her background picture. This way each person who sees her profile gets the subliminal message of her novel without her saying it all of the time.

The next thing that she does is 'direct' message someone. Sometimes you need to send a private message to a person away from the eyes of all of your followers. Sometimes a direct message makes a stranger feel more at ease. Of course, if they choose to answer you publicly you can feel free to post your response.

Just like Facebook, tweeting takes time but not as much time as you might think. Tweeting takes about the same amount of time, or less, than brewing a single cup of coffee. You can tweet throughout the day, but most people are not tweeting all the time. There are peak hours. Those hours are 8am-10am and then 5pm-9pm. So you don't have to tweet for six hours a day, but you want to hit the peak hours, even if it is just one or two tweets a day. Try to make it a habit so that people will begin to see you as an online presence.

Living on Other People's Web Sites

If someone Google's your name or book title, you want them to get a long list of results. To make that happen, you need to maximize your Internet presence. So if one Web site is good, several is better. The problem is that every site you set up will probably cost you money. Plus, designing, building, and maintaining several sites could get time consuming. Luckily, you can get additional sites for free and get someone else to do part of the work. Believe it or not, there are people out there who are eager to give you Internet space to showcase your novel.

Several sites now present a large collection of writers and their work. In my opinion, Author's Den (www.authorsden.com) is the leader of this pack. Various authors have posted more than nearly 380,000 titles on Author's Den. The template is pretty typical, and may be the model for other sites. You, the author, establish a free account. Then you can upload a photo, bio, short stories, articles, and a schedule of all your signings and other appearances. If you take the same care with this writing as you did for your main site, your Author's Den pages can be pretty impressive. You can see mine at www.authorsden.com/austinscamacho.

Of course you can upload your books, with a synopsis, an excerpt, and any good reviews you've gotten. After you enter their ISBN your books are automatically linked to Amazon.com. This is typical of free author sites, which are funded by their commission for Amazon sales. And since you earn the same amount on Amazon sales through their site as you do any other time, everybody wins.

One word of caution: your Author's Den site is free, but the owners offer paid upgrades and want very much for you to use them. Be prepared for persistent and repeated e-mails prompting you to invest in the upgrades. In my opinion, the benefits are not worth the cost, but you may feel differently. If you agree with me, you will hear from the site promoters regularly.

If that is horrendous to you, remember that Author's Den is only one of the sites that will host your book for free.

Pod People Unite

POD doesn't only stand for printondemand these days. It is also short for an iPod broadcast, generally shortened to podcast. A podcast is an audio broadcast that has been converted to an MP3 file or other audio file format for playback in a digital music player or computer. Most podcasts contain a human voice telling a story, sharing some information, or doing basically what we do in a blog only verbally. In this way you can share your fiction in your own voice. Podcasts must be hosted just like your site and blog, and more importantly, people can subscribe to your podcast through RSS (RDF Site Summary, informally known as Really Simple Syndication) format, just like a news feed.

What that means is that once a listener subscribes, they will be alerted to every new podcast you post. If they're a serious IPod user, your podcast will automatically load into their device every time they plugs it into their computer.

What does that mean to you, the fiction writer? Well, it means that you can read your short stories aloud and others can hear them. Short stories can hook people into reading your novels. Or, you can read one of your novels in short segments and get people hooked on a regular dose, sort of like a radio serial from the old days.

Like most methods of spreading your message on the Web, podcasting is easier than it sounds. First, you'll need a microphone. I use the one that came with my computer. Then you'll need audio editing and recording software. I use a freeware program called Audacity (found at audacity.sourceforge.net) which I learned to use in about ten minutes. Then you just need a place to host your podcasts. You could post them on a site like Pod Hoster (<u>podhoster.com/</u>) for a small fee, like I did years ago. Or you could just as easily upload them to Facebook or, like me, put them on YouTube (XXXX) or lots of other places. And there's no rule that says you can't also post them on your web site, your MySpace page (if you still have one) or anywhere else. If you're a bit nervous about leaping into this, just pick up a copy of *Podcasting for Dummies* by Tee Morris and Evo Terra.

Just remember that the purpose of your podcast is to increase awareness of your books and attract an audience. So make sure the content is high quality and fun. Keep it to an easy length for listening to in one sitting—I think twenty minutes is about the ceiling. And don't forget to mention where and how people can find your novels. Think of your podcast as a small radio show, and you're the sponsor. Never forget the commercial.

The Trailer Park

This next part doesn't fit into my evidence-based marketing plan. I have seen no indication anyplace that having a video trailer for your book will increase sales. But for pure ego gratification, nothing matches getting a little movie made promoting your work.

There are companies out there that will try to tell you otherwise and will ask for lots and lots of money to make it happen. They will be happy to put music or a voiceover to your moving book cover, script a pitch to read over animation, or even cast actors to perform a scene from your book for hundreds or even thousands of dollars. You can see the low-budget trailer I bought for Blood and Bone years ago on YouTube at **tinyurl.com/cca6nmz** and the more expensive, more polished trailer for The Piranha Assignment at **tinyurl.com/bmv47sx**.

However, you can—and should—try producing your own video, starring you, explaining why someone would want to read your book. You can view my amateur promotional video on YouTube at **tinyurl.com/cn69n6o**. Then take a look at my second attempt, for Russian Roulette, at **tinyurl.com/btaxddr**. I'll bet you can do even better.

I have asked my Intrigue Publishing partner, Sandra Bowman to give you a tutorial on how to do it yourself:

Book Trailer's 101

Most authors want something that they can show to draw people in while they are standing at an event. I was drawn to an author's computer screen last year because I saw a blinking eye. Yes a baby blue eye was blinking at me and it had me a little scared but I had to go see what it was.

As I stood in front of the monitor, I realized that this author had probably spent a lot of money on this advertisement. After all it had real actors and had sound and music and...well it looked very professional.

I can do that, I thought to myself and since I love a competition I decided to out-do her. This author had NO idea what she had started.

So off I went. I wanted to see if I could come up with a decent book trailer for myself and just like the designer suits or dresses we want but can't afford I found alternative ways to get what I wanted without spending the amount of money that she spent. ($500 dollars to be exact)

I started out by looking on my computer and what do you know. If you have a computer that's less than 10 years old you probably have a Windows program that includes Movie Maker or Mobi creator or some similar product. If you have a Mac you likely have something even better.

Then you need real people. That's easy because who doesn't want to be a star, right? Ask your friends, preferably the ones that might look like your characters or have the same personality as your characters. Then come up with a script. If they are your REAL friends, they have already read your books hundreds of times (ok, maybe not hundreds but at least once). Then pick out the best scenes and practice how to act it out. A word of caution; it doesn't have to be exactly like the book, it can deviate a little bit but make sure to keep the meat of the book. Then you need a camera. Well maybe not a camera but a camera phone. My ANDROID takes the best pictures and videos and I won't give it up! All that is left is to make sure you don't run on too long. Nothing gets older than droning through a video that is longer than a couple of minutes. Your book trailer should be no more than 5 minutes. Remember, catch and release, just like the fisherman. Catch their attention and then release them. It will make them want to buy the book, or at the very least talk about it and show it off. Once you are completed and you have given credit where credit is due, post it to YouTube and everywhere else you can think of that will let you upload a video. Facebook, Twitter, LinkedIn, GoodReads are all great places to put it out there!

Video book trailers

Book trailers without live actors are quicker and easier to put together. All the same rules apply except you are going to use stock photos. What? You don't know what that means. Stock photos are photos that you see on BING, GOOGLE, MSN and all over the internet. Those are photos that people have taken and shared somewhere. Now here is the most important fact for you to remember. There is no need for you to pay for those pictures! People are spending hundreds of dollars on pictures that you can get for free. What's the catch? Credit. What? Credit....give credit where credit is due. If you get a picture from BING at the end of the trailer, you have to say, "images courtesy of BING" or if there is a name associated with the pictures you have to give credit "photo of woman in red courtesy of Jon Black Productions via BING". See it's easy. You get a free picture and Jon Black gets free advertisement from you.

Sure, if you feel the need to get the images from ISTOCK or any other place online, feel free to pay because they will have millions of images to choose from.

I did not pay for one image in the production of the trailer I made for The Ice Woman Assignment (tinyurl.com/d775bum). I found the pictures I needed on BING and GOOGLE and took some of my own with my ANDROID phone.

Everyone that saw it thought I had paid for the pictures and here's a secret, some of the pictures are of my real items. I just took a picture and saved them to my computer. It's really that simple.

Adding words and music to your book trailer is also easy. However you need patience, after all Rome wasn't built in a day and your book trailer should take you at least two or three days to make. Start with the images and put them in the order you want them to show. Next pick the music you want, but you will need to make sure to edit it down and for goodness sakes, no curse words should be in it. After that you can add the captions and credits.

Voila; you're done!

Now, if you use a program on your computer it will literally walk you through it. This is not rocket science and it shouldn't cost as much as a small car to get one done.

If you take your time, you will have a professional looking book trailer in less than a week and then you can give yourself credit at the end with your name flashing across the screen as Producer. After all, you want to see your name in lights, don't you?

Other People's Web Sites

You can spread your online presence without owning an additional Web page or joining a social media site. I've already mentioned trading links with other writers and related people. You should also be asking everyone you know well if they have a Web site. Check it out and, if it's appropriate, ask them to add a link to your site. Some folks like the idea of having an author as a personal friend, and it gives them some shared fame to have a link on their site to yours. Relatives should be an easy sell in this regard.

Remember, there is no such thing as too much visibility for your book.

Now that you've taken the easy paths, look around for local web sites. In my area we have www.nva.com (for Northern Virginia), which advertises local events and businesses. It was a kick to get a mention on that site, and your local Web sites may be just as willing to promote your book.

Now do a Web search for "free classified ads." You will be stunned at how many places you can enter a free one- to five-line ad with contact information. Refer people to your site, and you might be surprised when a sale appears out of nowhere. If none does, it didn't cost you anything to possibly raise awareness of your writing.

And don't neglect Amazon.com. Most POD and small press publishers sell books there, and many include Barnes&Noble.com, BooksAMillion.com, and others. If you are promoting an ebook you will find Smashwords of value as well. But in the ebook business there is a sales difference you need to be aware of.

I have had very good luck with Amazon's Kindle Direct Publishing. Their system lends itself to good marketing because it is very easy to give away books on specific days. It is easy to promote that kind of a giveaway through social media and in my experience it results in solid sales. And Amazon is the biggest ebook store on earth. However, the KDP program requires exclusivity – the only exclusive sales outlet I would use. And like all the other online sales outlets, it has its weaknesses. Check your listings on these sights regularly for accuracy. Bug your publisher if any of the following happen (and they've all happened to me):

Your book's cover mysteriously disappears.

Your book is suddenly listed as unavailable.

Your book is listed as "out –of stock."

Yes, it is a pain for publishers to fix these problems, but they can and will if you make it clear that it's important to you.

Amazon is the most visible place for people to post reviews, and you should encourage them to do so. People buy books that someone else liked, so these testimonials are excellent sales tools. You can also copy them to your own site's review page. I send a thank-you note to anyone who reviews my books, regardless of how much they liked my work. Once encouraged, these people can provide valuable word-of-mouth promotion.

Chat Up Some Fans

With a little time invested, you could make some valuable contacts. You could start by sending messages to newsgroups and mailing lists. If you post an article on rec.arts.horror, other horror fans may well respond to it. After a while, when you mention that something like the events in a recent movie happens in your book, you'll become a discussion leader.

The same applies to chat room visits. There are thousands of chat rooms, Facebook groups and Yahoo groups, each filled with like-minded people. If you write espionage thrillers and you're in the spy novel room, just take part in the conversation. If you write paranormal romance, get a conversation going on the Facebook Supernatural Thrillers Room. Don't think about selling books. Eventually, in the course of the chatter, it will slip out. The magic moment, after you've established a few friendships in that group, will come when someone says, "Wait, did you say you wrote a book?" That's when you send everyone over to your site. The next day, you can be a hero and offer all the visitors to that chat room a discount and an autographed copy.

It is the nature of the Internet that all these approaches can begin the nationwide or even international recognition your book deserves.

Austin S. Camacho

Virtual Book Tour: A Good Idea; Didn't

Work

A publicist I've known for years told me this was the next big thing, and I must admit that on the surface it looked like a surefire winner. Blogs are quite popular and many of them are very focused on a specific topic. The biggest blogs have huge followings and are opinion leaders for their readership. You could think of these blogs as the morning TV talk shows of the twenty-first century. So why not do a book tour of these blogs? As a guest blogger, you can be interviewed by the host or post information and reach a large audience who would be just a click away from ordering your novel.

This publicist explained that for a mere thousand dollars, she could set me up for appearances on any number of sites and blogs that featured crime fiction and mysteries. I could do this all in the comfort of my own home, sitting at my computer. It sounded like an easy way to get a lot of positive publicity.

Reality proved a bit different. Between January and July, I got interviewed on one site and have no reason to attribute any sales to that appearance. I terminated the agreement wiser but much poorer.

I still think the concept is sound, and may work for you if you decide to do it yourself instead of outsourcing. If you can settle on a specific theme that's a hook for your novel, you can search the Internet for sites and blogs that focus on your theme. For example, if your book features supernatural events, then any blog centered on the spirit world or even psychic phenomenon should welcome you, whether your novel is a romance, mystery, horror, or new age.

This marketing approach will require a lot of time and effort searching out the right sites and making connections with their owners, but the potential exists for a lot of sales. Just because I haven't made it work doesn't mean it couldn't work for you.

9. Your Marketing Tool Kit

A broad variety of items add up to your silent sales aids. You'll use them in your review package and any mailings and hand them out at events. Their primary purposes are to introduce you and your book and to help people remember you. You could get all these things created for you at a print shop. If you have a halfway decent printer at home, you can make most of them yourself. Either way, keep your marketing tool kit simple and well stocked.

My Card, Sir!

Business cards don't need to be fancy, but they do need to feature your name, book title or series title, e-mail address, and Web site or Facebook page. Other information is optional. Mine have the word "author" under my name and, since I have more than one book out, the words "Hannibal Jones Mysteries" are at the top. I've also included my address and home telephone number, because I am less concerned with privacy than accessibility. Cards are fairly inexpensive, so stock up. Or, get them for free as I do at www.VistaPrint.com.

As you might expect, I hand my card to everyone who will take one. Anyone who wants my phone number or e-mail address gets a card. I also drop a card into every piece of mail that leaves my house, including bills. After all, they always stuff the envelopes they send me with advertising, and you never know who might be looking for a good mystery.

Make Up a Bookmark

Cards are perfect to give to bookstore managers, but the managers like to give bookmarks to their customers, so I supply them with bookmarks as well. Again, you can get these printed nicely for small money, but early in my writing career I chose to print my own, five to a sheet on eight-and-a-half-by-eleven-inch sheets of 67-pound card stock. I had a picture of one book cover and a short synopsis on one side. When I published a second book I put the same for it on the flip side. There was a space on the end where I would put "available at" and the name of the bookstore nice enough to hand them out. Of course, my Web site address was on every bookmark along with the title, my name, the publisher, price, and ISBN. If you choose to do it yourself, make sure you use a real paper cutter to separate them.

Some people laminate these things but I'm way too lazy. Some folks cut them smaller, but I prefer the two-by-eight-and-a-half-inch size. Your bookmarks don't have to look like mine; they just have to show some creativity, be attractive, and promote your book.

Sticker Fun

You'll need to order a few rolls of stickers, the kind that peel off easily so they won't damage your books. First, get some that say "Unedited Galley." These go on the books you send to reviewers to reassure them that they've received the book before its release date. You'll also need some that say "Autographed Copy" for the books you leave behind at bookstores after a book signing. These make the book more appealing to collectors. Other helpful stickers say, "Local Author" or, if appropriate, "Local Author, Local Setting." People like to support local writers, and they also like to read about places they are familiar with. You'll be surprised how effective these little gummed salesmen can be. Bookstore managers tell me that after a book signing, the remaining books sell much faster with these stickers than without.

Cover Photo

If you ask newspapers or magazines for reviews, send their art department a picture of your cover, preferably four by six inches. Newspapers appreciate anything that keeps them from having to scan or set up and photograph your book. Better yet, send an electronic copy of your cover. If that's your plan, make sure it's 800 dpi, so it will have sufficient resolution to reproduce in the publication.

You might also like to get color copies of your cover to hand out, much as you would bookmarks. And if you're going to have color covers printed up, you may as well go the extra mile (well, a few extra dollars actually) and have the other side printed as a postcard.

Full size pictures of your book cover could be useful as a response to the popularity of ebooks. More and more often at events people say, "I don't buy paper books anymore. I'll download one when I get home."

Of course, it's much better if they download it while they are at your event. To encourage that, I recommend you learn about QR codes, those little square designs you see everywhere. When someone holds their IPhone, Android or other smart phone over the code it will take them directly to the URL you choose. Naturally you'll choose the web page where they can download your book. It's easy to figure out how to create the codes at QRcode.com. You should put them on your brochures, bookmarks or any other handout you offer. This way, when someone promises to download your book when they get home, you can politely suggest they do it right then for the signing.

But, you say, you can't actually sign a Kindle or Nook version of your novel. True. But once you can see the book on someone's device you can sign and personalize the back of a book cover for them.

If they don't have their Kindle with them, you should have yours. Then you could actually "sell" them the ebook, and gift a copy to them. Once the book is in their Kindle account you sign the cover photo just the same as if you had sold a paper book.

Review Sheet

As you accumulate reviews and testimonials, you'll want to print them on a page together to hand out to people. Formatted properly, two reviews can fill a sheet and look impressive. As the numbers grow, you will squeeze more and more of them together and, eventually, you'll be faced with the wonderful task of choosing which comments are the weakest and will be dropped from your review sheet. One of mine is below:

"The Ice Woman is one of those rare books that does a lot of things and all of them well. Austin Camacho's sizzling tale smoothly blends action-adventure with the paranormal in a book that rivals Stephen King's Firestarter or John Farris' The Fury for power and relevance. As blisteringly original as it is wondrously structured, The Ice Woman is a one-sitting read that is not to be missed"--Jon Land, bestselling author of Pandora's Temple

Please believe me, after you read the next chapter, these things will come to you. Don't ever make them up, and don't ever use one without the person's permission. It will come back to bite you. A word to the wise, and all that.

Write a Killer News Release

You'll need to announce the great news about your new novel to the world. Initially, your release will go to news outlets, which will view it as incoming news rather than an advertisement. You can then use this document practically forever when you send your book out for reviews. After all, it's news to the person receiving it. With gentle rewriting, the release can go out each time you appear at a public event as a writer.

Media outlets have definite expectations of news releases. First, they expect them to be double spaced and one page long. Period. If you go over one page, those pages are sure to get separated, and someone has to search for it or guess what else was said.

Either way, you won't make friends with a multi-page release.

The format is pretty standardized. The words "For Immediate Release" go in the upper left corner, and contact information goes opposite that on the right. If you have letterhead paper, print your news release on that and add the contact information on the right.

Make sure the title of your release is as powerful as possible. Be bold and convince the recipient that what he's just picked up is real news. Then follow that headline with an interesting synopsis. If your release is going to local people or media, stress that you are a local author. If your story has a local setting, stress that as well.

Once you get some reviews under your belt, you'll want to rewrite your press release with the addition of the best sentence from a good review. A quote from someone else multiplies your credibility. Some experts favor quoting themselves in a news release, but my media contacts tell me they see that as the mark of a beginner.

You might want to add a little information about yourself at the bottom of the release. I prefer to send a separate full-page bio that includes a small photo of me. Figure 4 is a sample news release, and figure 5 is my bio.

I've also seen the recommendation that releases should note that the author is a great interviewee and is available for contact from media. If that is your style, go for it. I prefer to contact the newspaper or radio producer by telephone.

This is an appropriate time to mention another bit of subtle camouflage. In most cases, your vanity press or POD publisher won't send out releases for you. Some do offer this service for a fee, but you still have limited control and numbers. Small presses often leave news release duties to the author as well. An author sending out his own press release can seem a bit self-serving, so if you have a spouse or good friend who is willing to help out, list that person as your publicist or, my favorite, your branding manager. I like that term because hardly anyone outside the business knows what a branding manager does. It can be even more effective if that person is also willing to call newspapers or write to on line outlets that receive your release to follow up on it and offer you up as an interview subject

.

Fig. 4

For Immediate Release Contact:

Date:
Name:
410-490-XXXX
Email

Local Suspense Novelists Converge on Cambridge, MD

Mystery, suspense and intrigue will invade the "Place on Race Café" at 421 Race Street in Cambridge, Md., on Saturday, Oct. 26, from 10 a.m. to 4 p.m.

K.S. Brooks will read from and discuss her action adventure spy thriller *Lust for Danger,* and Austin S. Camacho will do the same with his mystery, *Blood and Bone.* There will also be time for questions, discussion and a great cup of coffee at the espresso bar.

Authors Brooks and Camacho are in the midst of a whirlwind book tour, in the last month just having completed featured appearances at the Baltimore Book Festival, Fall for the Book Festival, and at The Trover Shop on Capitol Hill. Camacho's new mystery *Collateral Damage* is scheduled to be released in November. Brooks recently signed a contract for representation of the screenplay for *Lust for Danger* to the cinema industry.

For more information on these free upcoming author events, visit the events pages at www.ksbrooks.com and www.ascamacho.com.

Camacho and Brooks are available for book signing events, lectures and media interviews. Mr. Camacho has been writing for over 15 years and is an Armed Services radio and television personality, while Ms. Brooks has been a writer for over 20 years and is also an award-winning freelance photographer. More information is available about the authors respectively at www.ksbrooks.com and www.ascamacho.com.

For more information, contact Name, branding manager for K.S. Brooks, at (410) 490-XXXX.

Fig. 5

Austin S. Camacho
Author • Journalist • Public Affairs Specialist

Austin S. Camacho is the author of five novels in the Hannibal Jones Mystery Series (including The Troubleshooter, Blood and Bone, Collateral Damage, Damaged Goods and Russian Roulette) and four in the Stark and O'Brien adventure series (The Payback Assignment, The Orion Assignment, The Piranha Assignment and The Ice Woman Assignment). His short stories have been featured in four anthologies from Wolfmont Press, including Dying in a Winter Wonderland – an Independent Mystery Booksellers Association Top Ten Bestseller for 2008 - and he is featured in the Edgar nominated African American Mystery Writers: A Historical and Thematic Study by Frankie Y. Bailey.

He is also a public affairs specialist for the Department of Defense. America's military people know him because for more than a decade his radio and television news reports were transmitted to them daily on the American Forces Network.

He was born in New York City but grew up in Saratoga Springs, New York. He majored in psychology at Union College in Schenectady, New York. After three years, he enlisted in the Army as a weapons repairman but soon moved into a more appropriate field. The Army trained him to be a broadcast journalist. Disc jockey duties alternated with news writing, video camera and editing work, public affairs assignments and news anchor duties.

After leaving the Army he continued to write military news for the Defense Department as a civilian. Today he handles media relations and writes articles for military newspapers and magazines. He also teaches writing classes at Anne Arundel Community College and is deeply involved with the writing community. He is an active member of Mystery Writers of America, International Thriller Writers, Sisters in Crime, American Independent Writers, is a past president of the Maryland Writers Association and past Vice President of the Virginia Writers Club.

This same reasoning applies to book clubs you might send your release to, and could result in you visiting that club during one of their meetings.

The Ultimate Brochure

Whenever you make a personal appearance or write to someone who should get more than your card, you'll want a giveaway piece that really sells you. Flyers have their place, and I believe that place is taped to the inside of a bookstore window. I've worked in the public affairs arena long enough to know that seldom does anyone take an eight-by-ten sheet of paper home to read. When we in government circles want someone to take home some useful information we give them a specialized brochure called a trifold.

A trifold is cool for several reasons. It goes in your pocket. It stands in a nice holder you can put next to the bookstore cash register. It separates information into discrete packets. It lends itself to color and design originality. Finally, has a writer ever handed you one before? See? It makes you different. My current trifold is reproduced, slightly shrunken, as figures 6 and 7.

It might look tricky, but I found it easy to build the six-panel trifold in the program my computer came with for designing newsletters. If you want to employ my formula, you'll include everything you want people to know. The front panel holds the book cover, title, author, and Web site address. As you open the trifold, you see a synopsis on the left and reviews on the right. The center inside panel has information about my hero. If you write horror, this might be about your villain instead. If you write science fiction or fantasy, maybe details of your fictional universe are in order. Anything that gets readers involved with your book is good. The other inside panel is my bio with a photo. The back panel is a pitch for my other novels. When I only had one book, the back panel held a small cover photo and details of where to buy a copy.

You can get pretty creative within this formula, and don't be shy about taking up space with appropriate royalty-free pictures you find on the Internet. I'm pretty sure my trifold has sold more books for me than any other passive marketing aid.

10. Get Reviews

A review is an evaluation of your book, a critical statement that rates its value. An endorsement is more of a testimonial just extoling the positives of your book. A blurb is generally shorter than a review or an endorsement, the few words of praise that you often see on the back cover of a book.

Good reviews, testimonials and blurbs not only convince readers to buy your book, they also convince booksellers to take a chance on it. They cause other writers to treat you with a little more respect, encourage your publisher to support your efforts, and show your friends and relatives they're not doing you a favor when they decide to read your book. In other words, these are very good things to have.

For the purposes of this book, I will not distinguish among blurbs, endorsements, and reviews. Personally, I use them interchangeably. Let people give you whichever they want to give you, and use them however you see fit.

When most people think of reviews, they think of major newspapers and magazines. I suggest you go there last. There are lots of other places to get some nice comments about your writing.

Who to Ask

Start by flipping through your mental Rolodex. Who do you know who has a small amount of fame, even locally? A politician? College professor? How about other authors who have already published commercially? All these people would probably be happy to read your book and write you a little blurb. If it's a friend or close associate, you probably won't have to give them anything more than a free, autographed book.

Also consider the manager of the bookstore you most often frequent. If you've formed a relationship as you left major chunks of your paycheck in his store, he'll probably feel honored that you want him to read your book and comment on it. This could pay extra dividends. Aside from the fact that people will assume that "Joe Jones, owner of Bestest Books" is an expert on good reads, if he likes your work Joe will become an advocate for you, and you'll never have to wonder where you can set up a signing, especially if you put his comments on the back cover of your book.

The next great sources of kind words are your information sources. If you write crime fiction, science fiction, adventure, or spy thrillers you have undoubtedly had to pick someone's brain at some time about the science, locations, tools, or techniques used by your heroes. These people are triple-good sources. They already like you, they know your book is well researched, and their expertise gives their endorsement credibility.

I have had a few of these people say, "I don't know how to write a review or blurb." This shouldn't be an issue. Give them your book for a final fact check (you should anyway), and ask them to send you an e-mail telling you what they think. Somewhere in that e-mail will be a couple of sentences that make great book blurbs.

If you've ever taken a writing course, don't overlook the instructor as a good review sources. Again, their expertise gives them instant credibility. If "Jane Gray, Chair of the Creative Writing Department, Xavier's School for Gifted Children" says your book is well written, most people will assume she knows what she's talking about.

You should ask every person you know who has a copy of your book for an endorsement. Every time I sign a book in person, I hand the new fan my card and remind them that my e-mail address is on it. Then I add, "As a local author, I love getting feedback from my neighbors, so when you finish my book, please drop me an e-mail and tell me what you thought." When I get an e-mail from readers, I immediately respond with thanks, and another request. Would they be willing to post a few words, much like what they already said in their e-mail, at Amazon? Or BN.com? Or, better yet, on Goodreads. It's their chance to be published someplace, with their name on the Internet in print. I'm frankly stunned at the quality of most of the reviews I have on Amazon, (over 170 at last count, spread over 9 titles.) When other people see that so many readers felt moved to write, they are more likely to purchase their own copy. And, of course, I lift those reviews for my review sheet and other promotional uses.

Now we enter more challenging but more effective testimonial territory. Whatever your genre of fiction, there are bound to be authors you admire. A blurb from one of them is like gold. If Tom Clancy says he likes your technothriller, most of us will buy it without another thought. But if Tom's not a close, personal friend. How do you get him to write, "Don't miss this great read"? Well, it will take some time, some patience, and a good deal of persistence. But it will be worth it.

Of course, you could introduce yourself to the author face-to-face. I met Warren Murphy at Book Expo America, told him how much I liked his work on the Destroyer series, and handed him a copy of *Blood and Bone*. A few weeks later I received an e-mail with a compliment. When I asked if I could use his words as a blurb for my book, he said "not a chance"... and wrote me a much better one!

Likewise, I met Ken Bruen at the Love Is Murder conference. Ken was born and raised on the Emerald Isle, so when I told him that two of my novels featured an Irish jewel thief he was happy to give the books a read. It was great to have a truly qualified crime writer verify that I got the Irish character right.

Failing a personal meeting, I recommend checking out the author's Web site. If there's no direct contact information, you can contact his publisher. If you don't get a response, look for a publicist's or agent's name on the site. If all else fails, write to The Author's Guild. Most popular writers are members, so the guild will have current contact information. Send your request to staff@authorsregistry.org.

From there it's just a matter of sending the author a short, polite request. Mention your favorite of their books and tell them why you liked it so much. If they inspired you or if their writing inspired some part of yours, tell them. Introduce your book in a couple of sentences and ask if they are willing to read it with the possibility of writing a brief endorsement if they like it. Send along backup materials, such as your bio, a brochure and any positive comments you already have, to prove that you're serious about this writing thing.

Your Review Kit

When you send a book out hoping for a review, don't send it alone. A package of supporting material makes it all much more impressive. As important as this package of materials is, you shouldn't have to reinvent any wheels here. Along with your cover letter, send your news release, your card, a bookmark, your bio, the photo of your cover, your review sheet, and a copy of any articles written about you. If that doesn't convince this writer you're serious, nothing will. You should also include your email address and if you're ambitious, a postage-paid envelope, so that the recipient doesn't have to make any effort to send back his kind words.

Over time I've polished my review package to an absurd degree. I put all the materials into a two-pocket folder in the order in which I want the recipient to read my stuff. My card is stapled to the front of one of the pockets so that if all else is lost the reviewer will be able to find my contact information.

Once you've mailed off your package, sit tight. A reply can take an agonizing length of time, but it's sure to come. I've never had a package like this ignored, although I have gotten back polite rejections. Publicists often reject review copies, and authors will sometimes legitimately plead a lack of time. But keep at it and you will bag a nice blurb from someone.

Star in a Local Publication

Now it's time to pull out that list of local magazines again. You'll also want to make a list of local newspapers. If you want to go statewide (hey, you decide what's local), 50States.com maintains an up-to-date list of newspapers with links to each one. For instance, www.50states.com/ news/utah.htm provides a list of Utah newspapers including all contact information.

Before you mail a package to any newspaper or magazine you haven't read, it's worth your time to give the publication a call. First, find out if anyone on staff writes book reviews. Don't expect any interest in writing a feature article about a fiction writer unless you have something pretty special in your background. You'll only set yourself up for disappointment.

Once you've established that there is a book editor, write your cover letter directly to him. It can be the same basic letter you sent to authors minus the paragraph on how much you liked their work. Instead, make sure you point out the local angle, specifically mention the enclosed review copy (in case someone else opens the mail and really liked your cover) briefly introduce your book, and ask for a review. Also mention in your letter what format your book is available in. For most of you that will be trade paperback and ebook, but if you have a hardcover out let them know. There is no reason to mention that it is a POD book or that you self-published or that your publisher is a small, local press. Half the local reviewers have never heard of POD and the rest have a generally negative opinion of "self-publishing." And yes, I know that good books do get self-published, but reviewers generally won't find them. And a special note for POD authors: you and your publisher may think you're different, but you won't make that sale to any professional reviewer. As far as the rest of the world is concerned, if you paid to make it happen, it's self-publishing.

Some small things can make your request a little more attractive to a local reviewer:

- Sign the book.
- Clearly label the envelope your package arrives in with the words "new book, review copy."
- Enclose a short handwritten note reminding the reviewer about the "local setting, local author" angle.
- If the office is within easy driving distance, hand-deliver the package, make eye contact with the reviewer and shake his hand. If you get this opportunity, explain that you don't expect a rave, but you know he'll be fair and honest.
- If you mail your package, call the newspaper or magazine in a few days to verify that it arrived.

Praise from the Pros

Now that you've mastered the basics, it's time to go for the big-time reviews. Appendix B is a list of the national publications that are kingmakers with their reviews. Some may not read POD or self-published books. However, considering the luck some of my fellow authors have had, most publications don't pay that much attention and I figure their policies may change before you throw this book away.

I've also included a list of individual reviewers, and encourage you to search for online reviewers. Scribe's World and Blether Book Review were the first two to review my books. Scribe's World is gone, but I still treasure those early reviews. I also most heartily urge you to send your book to Midwest Book Review. It is the only reputable reviewer of which I am aware that actively favors POD books and self-published books.

The rest of the publishing world wants to review books in advance of their release. So, when you print your next book, I suggest you do as I did and not sell any for four months. I know that sounds hard, but it can pay good long-term benefits. That means that when your publicist or branding manager calls the reviewers, she can tell them the release date, which should be four months in the future. When the concept of release date is introduced, the reviewer probably will never think to ask if your book is POD or self-published. Of course, the real reason for the call is to find out who at that publication reviews books in your genre. You want to send your review package to a specific person.

To continue the camouflage, have some stickers printed up that say "Unedited Galley." The galleys are the rough books traditional publishers send to advance reviewers. Theoretically, the galleys are what the author uses to proofread his book before the printer goes into final production. In reality, publishers do an actual print run of galleys to send to reviewers. Receiving galleys helps reviewers to believe they are getting advance copies of a book. It also causes them to ignore any typos or printing gaffs they may see. If I hadn't held *Collateral Damage* until its future "release date," I'm pretty sure I would not have gotten a mention in *The Library Journal*. It was certainly worth it to get that recommendation because this is such a prestigious publication it influences store managers as well as libraries.

Whenever you send review copies to a publication, you then need to watch that publication closely. Most reviewers won't call you up to let you know they're going to say something about your book, although the *Newport News Daily Press* actually e-mailed me to tell me that my review and book cover would be in that Sunday's paper. If you spot a review of your book, don't forget your manners amid the celebration. Send a thank-you note after every review, good or bad. No matter what, it's valuable exposure. And, either way, you want that person to be predisposed to reviewing your next book.

What if you send someone a review copy and never see a word in print? Don't give up. Cook up a new news release every month about what you're doing or capitalizing on a news event that ties in to your book. If you convince reviewers that your novel will remain timely, you might get a review in the future. And it will certainly make you harder to ignore when the next book comes out.

11. Publish Your Newsletter

I've learned that a certain percentage of the people who buy my books become fans of Hannibal Jones and will actively promote my work if given a little incentive. I keep in touch with those folks by making them a part of the big Hannibal family, and their common link is my newsletter. I don't make sales directly through my newsletter, but by constantly reminding my core audience of my work, I prompt them to promote me and that has led to sales. It also made a big difference to the opening sales of my second novel. Here was a market already prepped and actually eager to see the next book.

Who Gets My Newsletter

My electronic newsletter mailing list began with friends and family. Then a few coworkers showed interest. Today I have a list of nearly 700. You may choose to publish a paper newsletter. Your computer probably came with software to build one. I use that same template to print my trifolds. You can make it as colorful and fun as you like. I know from the experience of others that this can be very useful. It is also fairly expensive, so I've chosen to stick with an e-mail newsletter. There's no postage charge, and almost everyone I know would rather get e-mail than snail mail anyway. I use the template provided by Vertical Response, but Constant Comment and other companies offer user-friendly templates as well.

Everyone who e-mails me is added to my list. I am often at events with other authors and vendors. They all have business cards to hand out, and I add them to my list as well. I know authors who ask at their personal appearances and signings, "Would you like to be added to my mailing list?" This is a good idea, since people who opt into a list are less likely to drop out, although I haven't had anyone yell at me because my newsletter turned up in their e-mail. Of course, I do have an opt-out link clearly displayed on it.

I also add the e-mail addresses of the bookstore managers anywhere I sign. In the case of the occasional chain store, it could be the community relations manager. They may as well know that I'm still around, still writing, still making appearances at lots of other places.

And let's not forget all the other authors I've come to know through the writing associations I've joined, through the publishers I've worked with, and through meetings at conferences and conventions. Other writers are some of your most valuable centers of influence. They will almost always encourage people to attend your events, visit your Web site, and read your books. You should keep them posted about your progress.

What Do They Want to Know?

Just creating a newsletter won't get you far. Your newsletter needs to be interesting, useful and fun or no one will read it. To get the idea, I suggest you take a good look at what other writers are sending out. Mystery author Brad Parks produces my favorite writer's newsletter, and Rick Robinson's is another good example. You can sign up for my own newsletter at my web site, www.ascamacho.com.

When you're sending out a newsletter you need to know your audience. Remember, you're writing for them, not your own ego. If you know who your readers are you can write what they're curious about and interested in.

And remember that less is more! Most people prefer short emails and the same goes for newsletters. Follow the example of other writers, but however long your newsletter is, make sure it's packed with interesting and useful content. That "value added" content is what will hold your readers.

Try to keep your newsletter simple and easy to read. Sure you can get all sorts of color and pictures on there, but that can make it harder to read your message if your reader is using his or her phone. The system I use offers a full color fancy email, but it also goes out in a words-only version.

Readers today like to scan pages more often than they read deeply. Make sure you appeal to people who just want to hit the high points by writing strong headlines. You might want to make good use of bullet points. At the very least, write short paragraphs and leave plenty of white space on the page. Make it easy to get your messages without sifting through big blocks of copy.

How often should a newsletter go out? Well, that depends on how often you have news. In general I think that anything more than once a week will be regarded as spam. Longer than monthly and you risk being forgotten.

Remember that people are judging you as a writer by your newsletter so edit it carefully. Typos or bad spelling send the message that you don't care about your writing. And by the way, that same reasoning applies to emails, blog posts, and everything else you write. If you can't get a newsletter right, why should people think you can handle a short story or novel?

They're also judging you as a person, so don't overdo the promotion. A newsletter filled with self praise, special offers and blatant sales copy will lose you readership quickly. Of course the newsletter is meant to promote your books, but you need to balance that kind of content with useful information.

You'll want to tell readers what you're doing and give them the latest news about your writing, but some sort of value-added content keeps people coming back.

That having been said, your newsletter's primary purpose is to promote your writing. Therefore, whatever publicity or marketing news you have, this is where you share it first. My newsletter always opens with a cute or witty observation, and then gets right into a report on my most recent public appearance and writing and publishing news, and ends with my upcoming schedule of events. If I'm due to appear on TV or radio, or if an ad for my books will appear anyplace, that news goes in. When I started a writing collaboration, that news was in the newsletter. And if I'm traveling out of the area, I always let my posse know where I'll be so they can contact me for a possible face-to-face meeting.

Your readers are also very interested in any publishing news that impacts you. Do you have a new agent? Are you negotiating with a publisher? Is Hollywood looking at your story? News like this helps your readers identify with you and share your triumphs. They can be connected with you far more than they are with John Grisham or J. K. Rowling.

For the same reason, you should share your progress on your next project in your newsletter. Readers want to know if you're whipping along toward the next installment in that sci-fi trilogy or if you've decided it will actually take you five full-length books to tell the whole story. I've been surprised at how quickly people will write in if I get stuck on a plot point or need an obscure piece of information to make a storyline work.

Your newsletter is also a fine place to point out, one at a time, all the neat things on your site. Always include your URL prominently on your newsletter in case someone has forgotten it.

Value Added

The most important rule of newsletters is the same as the rule for Web sites. You had better give people something of value if you want them to keep reading. If you're good at short story writing, you can include one (or attach one to the e-mail) as a free gift. Or you can post the story in some secret place online – maybe on your web site – and only share the URL in your newsletter. That will make those folks feel special.

This is also a great place to share character information not found in your books. This way, your newsletter readers actually get to know your characters better than those people who just bought the books. As previously noted, Hannibal Jones's girlfriend is a great Cuban cook. I've been collecting recipes for her to use, and I occasionally share them with the group in my newsletter. You might want to explain a bit more about how your heroine's spy network is set up or, if historical romance is your thing, then give your readers a bit more background about the place and time period your star-crossed lovers exist in.

Before the release of my first adventure thriller, *The Payback Assignment,* I ran the novel in my newsletter as a serial. Each issue contained one short chapter. Not only did this give my readers something of value for free, but it got me early feedback about the upcoming book and built a bit of anticipation.

Many of your most dedicated readers are frustrated writers themselves. Why not get them involved in something a little interactive? I love the idea of starting a story and inviting newsletter readers to write the next chapter. If you get that thriller started, and leave your hero in a pip of a cliffhanger, you can bet that many of your readers will get a kick out of cooking up a neat way out of it.

That's one idea that ties into another cool concept, the contest. Contests are a great way to get people to keep looking for your next newsletter. If you get a good idea for something like this, come up with a creative prize such as Amazon gift cards, tickets to the next big movie in your genre or some other goodies related to your writing.

I've also included essays on my genre, hard-boiled fiction, and had write-ups on my favorite authors. A popular feature has been my reviews of newly released books, letting my readers know whose work turns me on. I like to be able to say, "If you like my writing, you'll also enjoy…"

A good newsletter calls for some time and a certain amount of imagination. It doesn't matter if you decide that yours will be an annual, quarterly or monthly. It can even vary. I started out sending a newsletter the week before any signing event because I knew my readers were largely local at the time and I wanted to prompt them to come visit me. At times that means every week. At least they know I'm busily promoting my writing—which is what you should be doing.

So far, we've discussed techniques for getting your book noticed without your active participation at the eye-to-eye level. A good Web site, reviews, and a newsletter will move books, but nothing is as effective as your personal presence. It's time to get into action.

Austin S. Camacho

ACTIVE MARKETING

"Behold the turtle. He makes progress only when he sticks his neck out."

12. Hold a Reading

If you're going to promote your books, you will be arranging for people to meet you in person. In some cases, you will simply sit and sign your books for the reading public. This kind of event has been most effective for me, but not for every writer. On the best of occasions for many authors, they are expected to give a presentation. This is one of those things that is eagerly sought by most writers until the opportunity actually appears. Then they face the dreaded question: "What do I say?"

Fiction readings—A Different Animal

For the nonfiction writer, this is fairly simple to answer. Give the audience some useful information, a sample of what's in your book, and you're a hit. The purpose of most nonfiction books is to educate or inspire. If the speaker convinces you that he is an expert in a subject that interests you, you'll want to buy his book.

Most authors who are interviewed on TV or radio who are not nonfiction writers are celebrities. When Madonna writes a book or when Tom Clancy is on the air, people want to know about them, their lives, and how they came to write a book, not so much about the book itself.

For you, things are a bit different. Even if you've written the greatest thriller in history, folks won't sit still for a long talk on how you researched it. Nor will they attend your talk to learn about your family life. Both those areas are appropriate to touch on in your presentation, but they can't anchor it. Your talk should be hooking people on your book, not on you. Unlike the nonfiction author, your book's primary goal is to entertain. So, what do you talk about, and how?

Structure Your Talk

Time is your friend. No matter how intriguing you are, the average person's attention span limit is about forty-five minutes, so don't hold forth for longer than that no matter what. With luck your hosts will give you an hour, which gives you fifteen minutes to answer questions from your rapt audience.

Now, if you have done this for a while and have had some success, don't read my words and throw out what has been working for you. What I am presenting here is not THE way to do it, but A way to do it. I've created a simple structure for book readings for beginners, because I've learned that when you have a track to run on, things are a lot less scary because you know you're headed in the right direction and will reach your destination.

Remember that regardless of your genre all you really want your audience to know comes down to five words: "My book will entertain you." You'll spend forty-five minutes saying that by finding the best parts of your book and shining some light on them.

The actual reading should not take up the majority of your time. I recommend reading five or six passages, and each should take you no more than three minutes to read. After that, your mouth will start to get dry. The rest of the time will be spent talking about the passages and getting people involved in your story, your characters, your setting, or your theme.

You'll begin structuring your talk by answering this basic question: why would someone want to read my novel? I decided that my novel upheld the best traditions of the hard-boiled detective story. From there, I decided what those most important elements were. I chose the type of hero featured, the social environment, the type of characters you meet, and the kind of action you see. Examples of those four concepts taken from my book became four of the readings I used, thereby proving that my book fit the mold. I also chose a reading that would exemplify the theme of my book. And I figured I should open, as my book does, by introducing my hero.

I think you could structure a reading for any genre of fiction based on this simple formula. Certainly, it makes sense to open with an introduction of the main character and close with action. I'm not sure what the defining elements of, say, fantasy-fiction are, but I'm pretty sure that the world the author created (environment), the types of humanoids introduced (characters), and the kinds of heroes and/or villains they have are among them. Only you know what your book's theme is, but you should make it clear in your reading.

When I tried a dry run of this plan with a live (but friendly) audience, I quickly realized that I'd need to introduce myself. I also wanted to explain the title of my book. I also included a bit of history of my genre. This required a little research, but I think it cemented my position as an expert in my narrow field.

There is one more element of a reading that I feel is essential. I didn't want to appear too egotistical, but that's hard to avoid when promoting your own creation. The out for me was to promote someone else's work. This is not purely altruistic. When I tout another writer, I am on some level putting my work in that ballpark. When I say "Raymond Chandler is my hero," I'm implying that my work is following in his footsteps.

That, in an extremely fat nutshell, is my plan for structuring a book reading. What follows is the actual set of notes I use when I read from *Blood and Bone*.

The type is big with lots of space between sections so I don't lose my place as I go. Also, this is not word-for-word what I say. You don't want to memorize your reading; you want it to be fresh and spontaneous each time, and in your own words of the moment.

If you have a copy of my novel, you can even follow along. Feel free to use this couple of pages as an outline.

READING—BLOOD AND BONE

Good evening, everybody. Before I start, is everyone settled in and comfortable? Good.

My name is Austin Camacho, and I'm here tonight to tell you about my first published novel, *Blood and Bone*. I'm a local author, living in Springfield, and I appreciate you coming out to hear about my book.

So... what is the book about? It's a locally set mystery, a real "who-done-it," with clues scattered about leading to a big finish. The ending should be a surprise, which makes reading from it a bit more of a challenge than I expected.

Mysteries come in different genre—from the tea cozy to the police procedural with plenty in between. My novel is hard-boiled fiction, the form I think was invented by Dashiel Hammett in the 1920s, and perfected by Raymond Chandler. This kind of thing requires first and foremost a hard-boiled hero, living in a gritty world. In this case, his name is Hannibal Jones and his world is Washington, DC.

Read intro (pages 1-3)

The Continental Op was the first hard-boiled detective, in Hammett's short stories. Then came

Sam Spade (he appeared in only one book and a couple short stories). Dashiel Hammett gave us FIVE books—*The Maltese Falcon, The Thin Man, Red Harvest, The Dain Curse*, and *The Glass Key*.

Hard-boiled also means exploring the friction that results in the meeting of poor and rich. Raymond Chandler made that his theme in San Francisco novels.

Chandler wrote SEVEN books including—1939's *The Big Sleep, Farewell, My Lovely*, and what I believe to be the best detective novel ever written: T*he Lady in the Lake*. You know his detective, Philip Marlowe.

Rich/poor interface here in Alexandria, just like San Francisco in thirties and forties. We have million-dollar townhouses within a couple of blocks of low-income housing.

(Setup)—In this scene, Hannibal and his girl (Cindy) meet a partner in her firm for a possible case.

Read getting assignment (pages 10-13)

My title—*Blood and Bone*—has two meanings. First, it's about leukemia. The teenager at the center of the story is being attacked by his own blood and bone.

But the title is also about family—as is my book.
(Setup)—In this scene the group goes to Mortimer's house, a huge place in Great Falls overlooking the Potomac.

Read meeting w/father (pages 17-19)

There are contemporary greats in the hard-boiled genre too. Elmore Leonard, Bill Pronzini, Robert B. Parker, James Elroy, and Walter Mosley are among my favorites.

Hard-boiled novels are about characters. The most important here is Kyle.

Read meeting w/Kyle (page 20-21)

Heroes in these books have a certain style—they must be heroes in a true sense.

Read page 25-26

If you read *Blood and Bone*, you'll learn who got murdered, learn what happens to Kyle, meet lots of other interesting characters, and follow the trail of Kyle's lost father and others who may or may not be related, up to Baltimore and all the way down to Mexico. Meanwhile, Hannibal solves a murder that takes place on Neiswand's property.

Before I go, I have to tell you that hard-boiled stories are about action.

(Setup) - pursuing a suspect in the murder I mentioned, Hannibal is beaten by gangsters and knocked out. In this scene he wakes up.

Read (pages 88-91)

I want to thank XX for inviting me to read tonight.
Thank you; you made this easy and fun.
I'm hanging around for a while.
I'll be happy to talk about the book, writing, myself, and sign copies.

Remember, it's a Performance

If you want your reading to be a big success, you must be entertaining. That means make eye contact with people and smile. Be animated. When you read dialogue, read it the way you heard it when you wrote it. Remember that not every character's voice is the same. Go ahead; indulge in a little acting. But you also must remember, that you are your own best asset; remembering the person you spoke to on the way in, shows that you are taking notice of the people who came to see you.

Be considerate of your audience and watch your language. Words that people are comfortable reading are not always words they want to hear aloud in mixed company. If you can't self-edit as you go, line out words in your book. You'll want to mark up one copy anyway. You'll want to clearly mark the beginning and ending of each passage you choose to read. In long sentences, I like to put marks where I'll want to take a breath. For goodness sake, put bookmarks in the pages to indicate the readings. And don't get arrogant or overconfident. I carry my notes with me and make no bones about looking at them as I speak. When you've practiced enough, you'll only need to glance down for a second to know what you want to say next.

If your audience is engaged you will get questions. In the beginning, ask everyone to hold his or her questions until the end. I take them as I go now, but if they get ahead of me I'm not shy about saying, "I'm coming to that in a minute. First I want to tell you…" and getting right back on track.

One more bit of advice, and this applies to all readings, signings, and other personal appearances. The more positive vibes you gather in your vicinity, the more fun you will have and the more books you will sell. So make sure you invite all your friends, family, and local supporters to every appearance you make. That way, you will have some supportive faces in the audience and you will never have an event at which no one shows up.

The Hardest Part—Show Me the Money, Please

Unless you're reading in a mainstream bookstore, you will bring your books with you. These will be books you have bought, and you will sell them yourself. For me, the least comfortable part of marketing my books is handling money. As Dr. McCoy might have said, "I'm an author, not a salesman." The best way to handle this, whenever possible, is to have a confederate accompany you. It really makes life better to be able to say, "Denise over there will take your money." Then you can concentrate on chatting with people as you autograph their books. It just feels more professional.

Make sure you have plenty of the right change. And carry a calculator to every event. You don't want to fumble when that lady says she wants three copies to use as gifts.

When I started doing readings and signings I had to disappoint some prospective readers because I was only equipped to handle cash or checks. Today, you don't need to let the credit card crowd down. If you have a smart phone you can order a device from Paypal for free that will enable you to swipe a credit card wherever you go. It's more than worth the trouble.

Okay, you're all set to do a reading. Now, let's find some places for you to do them.

13. Attend Book Fairs

If you want to be seen as an author, then you should go where authors go. That means appearing at book fairs and conferences whenever possible. For the purposes of this book, I have lumped events meant to appeal to writers together with those designed for the general public. These events all are opportunities to be associated with better-known authors, generate a little buzz, and maybe sell a book or two.

Participate...

A simple Internet search will give you the names and dates of book fairs in your own area. These events usually take place in the spring and the fall, and most will have their own Web site listing the details. In my area, springtime brings the Howard Community College Book Festival, the Bay to Ocean Writers Conference, the Virginia Festival of the Book, and Fall for the Book at George Mason University, in addition to conferences/book fairs held by each of the writers' associations to which I belong. Autumn brings the Baltimore Book Festival, Artscape, and the Random House Book Fair.

Even if you don't want to travel far enough that you'll need to pay for a hotel room, you shouldn't overlook the major multi-day events because many of them, like Book Expo America and Bouchercon, are held in a different city each year. And your publisher might offer its own writers' conferences. My previous POD company, Infinity, puts on a conference every year. And Intrigue Publishing, the small press I helped found, produces the Creatures, Crimes and Creativity conference annually (creaturescrimesandcreativity.com)

Contact these events as early as possible to ask if you can be part of the program. Your best bet is to be part of a panel of speakers. In my case, I point out that I am a mystery writer, that my novels are locally set, that I feature an African-American detective, and for writer-oriented events, that I have published through a POD publisher, self-published, and been published by a small press. I've just enumerated several different panels to which I could contribute. Include an autographed copy of your book with your request. This is that wonderful, rare instance when you will actually be judged based on the quality of your writing.

At my first Festival of the Book, I landed a panel spot alongside four other authors whose work is set in Virginia. We had a lively discussion, which I think was worth a lot in terms of credibility. Afterward, in a nice little area set up for author signings, people actually sought me out to tell me how much they had enjoyed our panel and, of course, to get a book. The bookstore working the festival had ordered several copies of my novels but I sold out, a nice feeling; considering the other authors I was there with. In later years I've been on panels with John Lescroart, Libby Fisher Hellman, and Lee Child, some of the most successful names in my genre.

It's even more fun to do a reading from your book. The Baltimore Book Festival has a "Next Big Thing" tent, which features local emerging authors. I was given a thirty-minute slot during which I read passages from *Blood and Bone* and answered questions about the writing process. Afterward, of course, there was an area set up for author signings.

It's a lot harder to get on the program of the national book fairs than it is to appear at local events, but it's not impossible. You will definitely want to find out if your publisher plans to have a booth at any of the publishing events. When Infinity set up a booth at Book Expo America in New York City, I let the company know I was willing to be there, and its executives realized it was to their advantage to have authors present to sign books. Most of the publishers give away hundreds of books at this event, and Infinity decided to join in, supplying a huge box of my novels for me to sign and give away. Of course I didn't make money there since there were no actual sales, but I think the appearance paid off in credibility and promotion. Many of the people who took my book home were booksellers and library workers, exactly the people I want to know my name. Ego boosting aside, I also met my much-published collaborator, Warren Murphy, and publicist Penny Sansevieri, who contributed to the volume you're reading now.

Over time I've attended Thrillerfest, Bouchercon and Love Is Murder enough times that I am automatically placed on panels. This has allowed me to build a small following in cities far from home.

Sign and Sell...

You can't always be part of the schedule at book festivals, but that's no reason not to attend. For example, the Maryland Writers Association's annual conference hosts a bookstore to showcase members' books whether or not those authors are speaking at the event. This is a great place to make some sales, especially if you happen to be sitting in that bookstore to sign books.

The MWA also rents booth space at a few local book events to promote the association. The organization always needs volunteers to staff those booths, and those volunteers are encouraged to sign and sell books there. Even when I wasn't reading at the Baltimore Book Fair, I had the opportunity to sign a few books at the MWA booth, as I did at Artscape. The Writer's Center holds a small press book fair each year and offers space to local authors that is very inexpensive. That fair has a place in my heart because it was the first event I ever attended. I signed my first book for a stranger there, and that's a feeling I'll never forget.

I've learned that small things make a big difference at these events. Naturally, you'll want to have many of the items from your review kit handy. You'll want to offer passers-by your card, trifold, bio, and review sheets. Bookmarks are very popular giveaways. If you've been featured in any articles, mount a copy on foam core board for all to see. A nice big poster of your book cover also is a good idea. You can get such items printed very inexpensively if you stick to the standard eleven-by-seventeen-inch size.

After about a year of watching other writers, I figured out the one thing that would have the greatest impact on sales. I needed one more poster. That poster features smaller versions of my book covers, but the important part is the lettering. It says "Author signing today. Austin S. Camacho, author of the Hannibal Jones mystery series, will be here today to sign copies of his novels." I put that sign up on a tripod, usually right behind me. I put a smaller version on the table in front of me to further reduce confusion.

I've now added a six foot tall vertical banner that unrolls from a compact container (you'll find them at

Banners.com.) It has a life-size picture of my face with my name under it and a statement that I'm "author of the Hannibal Jones mysteries and Stark & O'Brien thrillers. I still have people walk up to me, read the signs, look at the books, and ask, "Are you the author?" I occasionally wear a button that says "Hug me, I'm a writer," which does seem to help people discern my identity—not to mention netting me some nice hugs.

Or Just Attend

A POD author or one who is self-published is very unlikely to speak at, say, Bouchercon, and events like that don't provide much of an opportunity for little-known authors to sell books. That doesn't mean you shouldn't go. It's still a chance for some great networking, which can lead to sales down the road.

However, you will need to be outgoing and outspoken. Don't be shy about asking people what they write. When you find people in your genre, strike up a conversation. I've picked up some very valuable information this way, including which bookstores are eager to have author signings and the names of the owners or managers. Writers are often eager to help you out and spread the word about your work. You might also meet that author whose style is so compatible with yours that you want to share a signing or share a booth at some event that's cost prohibitive or just too intimidating for you to do it alone.

Display at BEA: A Good Idea That Didn't Work

One of the benefits offered by the Independent Book Publishers Association (formerly the Publishers Marketing Association) is the opportunity to display your book at Book Expo America, the Frankfurt Book Fair, and Library Association events. These are the places where the people who buy books for large bookstores and library systems look for new products. It is also where foreign publishers buy the rights to American books to print and sell overseas. These are huge events, and showing a book at them would appear on the surface to be wonderful opportunities. Other associations and companies offer similar opportunities.

A $350 investment placed my newest title on a shelf at BEA among a couple of dozen other mysteries and maybe a couple of hundred titles all told. Because I was at the expo, I spent a fair amount of time standing near my book, although few authors were actually present. I chatted with a number of acquisition editors and librarians, and exchanged cards with many of them. It was at least great fun and exposure I probably couldn't have gotten any other way.

But when all was said and done, I was not able to trace a single book sale to that event. Despite the benefit to my ego, my balance sheet calls this one a failure. I do know other authors who swear by these displays. I can only say that for me, this idea didn't pay off.

14. Explore Nontraditional Outlets

If you're like me, when you first thought of book signings, you thought of bookstores. That is the most obvious idea, but it is also the site of most of your competition. If you're determined that bookstores are THE place to promote your writing, then you can skip this chapter and get to it. However, my experience has been that a lot of other options have yielded better results. Give these ideas a try and after your first fifty-book signing you might come over to my way of thinking too.

The Local Library

The library may not seem very nontraditional, but it is regularly overlooked by authors. Your library is a most writer-friendly environment, and everyone there is there because they read.

Make your approach in person. Every library has someone responsible for special events. Find that person and ask how you might arrange a reading session. Don't be surprised if he asks to see your book. Hand one over, along with the same package of support materials you send reviewers. Then tell that person that you would like an hour to speak about your book and how you came to write it. Remind him of the local author/local setting angle.

At this point, you may be startled to be asked how much you charge for this service. Libraries often pay writers to speak, despite the fact that they never really have the budget for that sort of thing. Be honest and explain that you are a new author and that your primary purpose is to make your name and work more familiar in your home territory. You will ask two favors. First, that the library promotes your talk through its usual channels and put up posters and such to let people know you'll be there. Second, that you would like to be able to sign books after your talk. Rather than charging for your time, you would be pleased to make a donation to the library, say, 20 percent of the sales.

This approach worked quite well for me in Virginia. On the appointed evening or weekend afternoon you should find yourself faced with a small number of attentive and polite adults, ready to hear whatever you have to say.

Good or bad, don't forget to send a thank-you note to the person who arranged for your reading. They will probably order a couple of copies of your novel for the library, and may well recommend your work to the readers he knows.

Local Book Clubs

James Patterson probably has little interest in sitting with ten or twelve readers in hopes of selling a book or two, but for you and me, it's a fine opportunity.

My first experience in this area demonstrates how all this activity I've been recommending comes together. I was at the Maryland Writers Association booth at the Baltimore Book Fair when a young lady stopped to chat with me about my novels. Ultimately, she bought one (yay!) and mentioned that she was an avid reader, and member of an active book club. I asked if she thought her club would like to have an author come and speak at a meeting. She was thrilled at the prospect and promised to contact me. I nodded and smiled, but suspected a brushoff.

I was pleasantly surprised when two weeks later I received an e-mail telling me that she had enjoyed my book very much and recommended it as one of the club's reading selections. The next thing I knew, nine more books were ordered through my Web site. I signed them all and mailed them promptly.

The members met at a nearby Barnes and Noble store at 10 a.m. on Saturdays. They bought me coffee and treated me like a celebrity when I arrived. I brought bookmarks and brochures for all. While I had some prepared notes, I never used them. For forty-five minutes I answered some great questions about how I came to write that novel, why certain characters did the things they did, and what I was thinking when I wrote a particular scene. It was a joy to be surrounded by people who were so interested in my favorite subject—my novel!

Near the end of our time I introduced my follow-up book and each member asked for one. It's a good thing I brought enough with me, and had appropriate change in my pockets. I wondered briefly how the manager of that Barnes and Noble, who had refused to put a couple of my books on her shelves, would have felt about ten copies being sold in her meeting area without a penny going to the store.

So, let's see. Twenty books signed and sold, and ten likely word-of-mouth supporters for an hour's work, or actually, an hour's fun. I think that at those rates, book clubs are a good use of my time.

Coffee and a Book

I held my first reading in a local coffeehouse. It was a warm, relaxed atmosphere and the people there were very supportive. I had no expectations, so the number of books I signed was a pleasant surprise. Thirty books is a good total for any book signing, plus I made more of a connection with those who bought them. I recommend it to anyone as a wonderful early experience.

Now I'm not talking about one of these chain places where people grab their double-decaf half-foam skim cappuccino to go in the morning. To make this work, you need to have a traditional, owner-operated coffeehouse, the kind of place that survives and competes with Starbucks by being part of its community. You're looking for a place that occasionally hosts live folk music or displays the work of local artists for sale. It gets extra style points if it's named after someone, as in "owner's first name" Café. These establishments may also have nice, quirky names like some in my area: St. Elmo's Café or the Hard Bean Coffee Sellers.

Approach these places well in advance to see when they might have space in their schedules. Once you've been granted an hour, have a couple of window posters made advertising the day and time. Print a few of your trifolds with the day and time of your reading on the front under the picture of your book cover, and leave them at the coffeehouse for people to pick up. The idea is to make this an anticipated event.

By now I shouldn't have to tell you to send a release to all your local newspapers every month or so, promoting all your appearances and focusing on any news tie-in to your book. When you're at bookstores or libraries, you also need to send a separate notice to each newspaper's community events page. This might be called the Community

Bulletin Board or Coming Attractions or some such, but it is usually a weekly feature on Thursday or Friday, telling everyone what to do and where to go in the coming week. You generally get a one or two line notice on the order of:

"Austin Camacho will read from his mystery novel "*Collateral Damage*" at the Hard Bean Coffee House in Annapolis, Md., on Saturday at 1 p.m."

It may seem minor, but so many people have told me that they saw my name in the paper because of those little blurbs that it has given me a small amount of local celebrity status. Remember, generating buzz is the name of the game. It's part of your camouflage that makes you look just like a big-name author.

Your results will be a little better if you arrive a good half-hour early for a coffeehouse reading. It's important to get comfortable in the place. When the time comes, ask the manager to get everyone's attention and introduce you. At first, I wrote a short intro on a file card, but people seem happier when the manager says something very simple such as "This evening we're pleased to welcome Austin Camacho, a local mystery author who's going to tell us about his newest novel, *Collateral Damage*."

Make sure you've got a cup of the place's specialty in front of you. Thank your host, and ask if everyone in the audience has their coffee too before you start. Drumming up business makes the manager happy, and if the audience members have their drinks at the start, they are less likely to get up in the middle of your tense reading from Chapter 3.

I like to get away from the reading chair as quickly as possible after I'm done. I find a comfortable seat where I can be approached from as many sides as possible. People want to sit with you and talk about your book or ask questions. If the coffeehouse is taking a share of your sales, let the books go through its cash register so you can focus on signing and talking. And I recommend that you relax and hang around. I've signed four or five books half an hour after my talk was done when people have come in and said, "Was that book thing tonight?" Then they sit with me, enjoy some one-on-one time, and ask if it's too late for them to get a copy of that book.

Arts & Crafts, Etc.

You've been to arts and crafts shows, I'm sure, but have you considered working them? The folks who attend these events are usually there for the specific purpose of spend money. Amid the two-dollar spool dolls and two-hundred-dollar pieces of handmade furniture, the price of a book doesn't seem out of line. Besides, you'll probably be the only author on site, and that means your booth will represent a somewhat different option for gift shoppers. And what more personalized gift could there be than an autographed book signed, "To Bob, Enjoy the mystery!"

These events come in a variety of forms. There are subtle differences between being a vendor at crafts fairs, flea markets, wine festivals, music festivals, parades, and community festivals, but the basics are all the same. You can find out about these events by reading the newspaper and checking your local community Web site, but that way often you'll get the word too late to be a part of it all. I recommend you check a site like Festival Network Online (www.festivalnet.com), which bills itself as the "nationwide craft show, art fair, music, festival and event guide." These events are listed months in advance, allowing you to plan your promotional appearance schedule.

But now we push into new territory, because these events require both some planning and a certain amount of investment. Whether the event is indoors or out, you'll want a canopy for your booth space. The space you get is generally ten by ten feet, the exact size of most canopies. Make sure you get something that one person can put up and take down quickly.

You'll also need a couple of tables. Six-foot-long plastic tables are fine, although you might like one that folds in half after you fold up the legs. Having two tables allows you to set up to face two directions if you find yourself in a corner space or to add some depth to your display if you're just facing one way. I like to sit a small, two-shelf bookcase on the second table behind me or to one side. Add books to the bookcase and you've given your space some depth, making it more visually attractive. Hang posters from the top crossbar of the canopy behind you, and you're in a three-dimensional space that begins to look like a room.

Some events require tablecloths that go to the ground, so get a couple of solid color coverings that fit the bill. You also need a comfortable chair, and you'll probably need it more of the time than you expect. I've read manuals that tell you to stand as much as possible at book signings, and generally I agree. But my personal experience is that at some fairs and similar events, standing behind the table covered with display materials intimidates some people. If I back off a bit, and sit down, they are more likely to come up and pick up a book. I'm not likely to make a sale until someone reads the back cover of one of my novels or at least grabs a brochure. If you decide to exhibit at such fairs, try it both ways and see what works for you.

I will quickly point out that you must always remain open and receptive to people. While sitting back for a while might be okay, sitting and reading the paper or staring at your laptop is not. Even if they are interested in your books, people are naturally polite and won't want to interrupt you if you appear to be busy.

Invest in a few small stands that can hold a book so they stand facing outward, and a brochure holder or two for your tri-folds. These things are inexpensive at Office Depot or Staples. While you're there, grab a business card holder and a box of small plastic bags. These stores also have inexpensive quick-folding easels that are ideal for holding posters so people can spot you at a distance. I also like the small cardboard displays I have that hold a small row of books. Take a look at the options at places like www.bookdisplays.com and www.citydie.com to choose what looks great to you.

I have also purchased a standing banner – mine is from banners.com but there are lots of sources. The banner is 3 feet wide and stays in a pretty small reel from which it unrolls like a venetian blind to its full 6 foot height. It's big enough and bright enough to make me hard to miss even at a distance.

Finally, get creative with your display. If there are any items you think will be eye-catching and fit the theme of your books, put them on your table. A toy six-shooter, a sword or a laser pistol would tell people instantly what kind of story you've written. K. S. Brooks, author of the action adventure-spy novel *Lust for Danger*, puts defused hand grenades on her tables whenever she attends a signing. This never fails to draw people, and the question, "Why do you have these grenades on your table" offers an easy opening to talk about her heroine and her book.

The two ladies who write romantic adventure novels as C.C. Colee go to signing events prepared.

The trilogy about the rise of a woman pirate begins with *RB: The Widow Maker* and who wouldn't stop to ask questions when they see two lady pirates all dressed up standing behind their table? They also put out a pirate chest full of chocolate pieces of eight and appropriate figurines. They get my vote for best author display, they have a lot of fun at signings, and they move a lot of books.

Remember, there will be an investment for the space itself. The cost varies widely, from twenty-five dollars for an afternoon to more than five hundred dollars for a three-day, all-day event. Only you know how much attendance is worth to you. I rarely attend an event that will cost more than I can recover with twenty book sales. But keep in mind that the money you take in isn't the whole picture. The exposure, the newspaper listing in the community bulletin board, and the possible contacts all have value. And, believe it or not, people really will take your card and brochure away and place orders later.

Each time I sign a book in a public place like this, I tell the person that my card is in the book and ask her to send me an e-mail when she finishes the book to let me know how she liked it. Those flattering e-mails are easy to turn into additional sales.

Never just fill out a form and send in money for an arts and crafts festival. Always call and speak to someone. Explain your intent and verify that you are welcome. Some of these shows are juried art exhibitions designed to showcase the handwork of fine artisans. But even when they are advertised as that kind of show, I've sometimes been surprised by the reception. Sometimes the person I contact will say, "You wrote the books? Well then, it's your own work. Come on in." And sometimes, the reaction is, "Wow. We've never had an author in a booth before. That will really add something to the show!"

Flea markets are a little different in that you will usually find used as well as new items there. Ask if you can have that space that's a little apart from everyone else. Put up your "author signing today" signs and you will almost appear to be a separate event happening in the same place. And don't leave early. I've often made half my sales to the other vendors who did well and buy on their way out.

Music festivals, holiday parades, wine festivals, and community festivals usually have more going on, with a crafts fair being only part of the fun. Don't wear a suit and tie to these events. People in shorts and t-shirts will be uncomfortable talking to you. And remember to have a good time. It isn't all about money, you know.

If you think this is a silly or undignified way to market books, then you probably shouldn't do it. My experience is that almost everyone I see at any of these things is happy and pleasant, and people don't try to avoid me as they sometimes do in bookstores. My first fifty-plus book signing was at a wine festival. It seemed to be a fairly upscale crowd, but very relaxed and friendly. It started at noon, so I didn't have to get up early that weekend, and the festival was over at 6 p.m. Vendors received two commemorative wine glasses and although I didn't buy any wine that weekend, people kept pouring samples into one of my glasses so I could taste their latest find. That was a good time.

There are some other cool event possibilities that I can't even attend, but you might be able to. Every year, there are science fiction fairs, comic book conventions, renaissance festivals, anime conventions, and the like all over the country. If you happen to write fantasy or science fiction books, you might be very popular at one of these events. Plus, if that's the stuff you're into, then at the very least you should have fun there and make some friends.

15. Bookstores—The Final Frontier

Why have I left bookstores for last? Because creating a successful bookstore event is the most work, often for the least return. Because many bookstore managers have little interest in you, your book, or in hosting a signing. And because it's the only place I've signed books where I encountered downright rude customers.

However, there's no denying that there's more prestige attached to holding a moderately successful signing at a bookstore than is in selling out at a flea market. You don't have to haul tables, chairs, or a canopy to a site. And if your publisher has made connections with a distributor, you don't even have to bring the books. So, let's take a look at how to make the bookstore appearance work.

Between the yellow pages and the Internet, you can make a list of all the bookstores in the area. Be prepared to contact them all eventually. Most of the major chain stores will back away from you as soon as they discover that they can't order your books through their normal distribution chains or if they learn your books are nonreturnable.

You can avoid these conditions. Almost all POD publishers can put your books through Ingram or Baker and Taylor, the biggest national distributors. And while it may cost you extra, the publisher can make your books fully returnable too. In some cases this will only be a partial solution because some POD companies (and some small presses) only accept returns directly. Bookstore managers find it easier to both order and return books through their distributors. Even under those conditions, it will help a little to be able to say your books are returnable.

If you self-publish, be sure you make connections with one of the big distributors too. If you can't get a contract with Ingram or Baker and Taylor, there are several other distributors who may be willing to handle your books.

As a self-publisher you can also obtain your books from Lightning Source, a digital printer owned by Ingram. The company uses the POD process but books it produces are all available through the parent company.

If you do work with a small press, don't accept a contract with one that doesn't promise that your books will be fully returnable through a recognized distributor.

Even that won't guarantee you a signing. When a store manager goes to her computer and sees that the warehouse only has two of your books in stock, she will immediately know that they are self-published or published POD. How do you get past that to arrange a signing?

Making Contact

I believe in supporting privately owned bookstores, so I encourage you to start with them. The easiest way to find all the independent bookstores in your area is by doing a simple search on the American Booksellers Association site (www.bookweb.org). I check this listing frequently because new bookstores seem more open to setting up events.

For each store, call to find out when the manager will be in and when during that time business is slowest. I don't favor trying to establish anything else by telephone. If you have a persuasive person playing the part of branding manager or publicist, he may be able to establish a signing date by telephone, but in my experience, store managers think little of authors who call them to set up an event.

I have had very good results paying a woman I trust to be my publicist just for this function. I supply the list of bookstores, phone numbers, and a rudimentary phone script. She makes contact by phone and requests signing dates. If she meets reluctance, I mail the store manager a media kit, which is identical to my review kit except that it includes a copy of one of my novels. Then she makes a follow-up call. If you can find someone who will represent you well on the telephone, I highly recommend it.

Otherwise, call on the manager in person. No jeans or sneakers for this visit, although "business casual" is okay. Bring a small case with examples of your marketing tools and have a copy of your book in your hand. Identify yourself and ask to speak to the manager. As soon as she says hello, hand her your book. My opening is short and simple.

"I'm a local mystery author and I didn't notice my novel on your shelves. I'd like to schedule a book signing event in your store, so I stopped in to see when the best time would be."

Then I stop. You see, this person is about books, and right then she's examining mine. She's examining the cover art, reading the back cover, testing the binding, checking for an ISBN, glancing at the copyright data, and looking to see if the opening line is a hook that would draw a reader in. Her number one question is whether this looks like a professional book.

Once that is established, there are still standard objections. My favorite is, "We don't do book signings." That's when I make my one and only sales pitch.

"I could pull a lot of people into the store on a day/night like this. People like to talk to local authors and get autographed books. It makes you look good to support the local guy. If you have any difficulty getting my books in stock, I am happy to offer books on consignment. That means I bring the books with me and all you have to do is take the money and keep 20 percent of it. Doesn't that sound like something you'd like to do?"

If the manager can't see my point of view after hearing that I thank her and move on. In the beginning I wrestled for signings, but I soon learned that people who are really negative about the idea are terrible hosts and make for a miserable experience.

If the manager does get it, I lay out my plan, just as I'm about to lay it out for you. Then I ask what day and time would be best for our first reading. As soon as the time and date are established, I get out of that manager's hair and get to work building my event.

Follow Through

It is your obligation to make a signing a success, not your publisher's and certainly not the bookseller's. Securing success starts with advance publicity. Make sure you send a release to every newspaper and television and radio station in your area. Send a separate notice to the community bulletin board section of each newspaper. Post the upcoming event on your web site. Write it up in your newsletter. Send the notice to the newsletter editor of your writers' association. Mention it on Facebook. I like to make a Facebook event and invite all my friends who live within a reasonable distance.

In the meantime, be sure you order enough books far enough in advance to be well stocked for the signing if the store won't order them. Either order or make plenty of brochures and bookmarks. Add the name and address of the store, and the date and time of your reading to about fifty of your brochures and bookmarks.

Setting Up

Two weeks before your signing, it's time to visit the bookstore again. You need to make the environment more welcoming to you and get it oriented for your big success. Military leaders call this "preparing the battlefield."

You'll start by surprising the manager with the fifty bookmarks and brochures. You told her you'd be there with them, but she didn't really believe you because no one else has ever done anything like this. You'll put the brochures as close to the cash register as possible because nothing sells like "point of sale" material. You'll present her with the bookmarks and ask her to drop one into the bag with every purchase. Bookstores love to give away bookmarks, and their customers generally love to get them.

If there's space beside your brochures, put a copy of your book in an upright stand. Then ask where in the window is best for your posters. You want at least one of your "author's signing" design but instead of saying "today," it should list the date and time of the event. Then go over to the appropriate section of the bookstore and post three or four more copies of your book. They should be arranged so the front cover faces out (instead of the spine) and they should be wearing removable stickers that read "local author." Don't worry about money at this point. Unless you're in an extremely small bookstore, their cash register will tell them every book of yours they sell by the bar code.

During this visit, establish where you will sit during the signing and which way you will face. You don't want to be in the way of traffic, but you do want to be where everybody who enters the store will see you. Don't be shy about expressing your preferences. Most store managers don't really know how to host a book signing. They expect you to be the expert and want you to be proactive.

Showing Up

Be a little early, but don't haunt the store. You want to make an entrance, just in case there are people who might be waiting to meet an actual author. If there's space, put your "author signing today" poster on a tripod next to you. Switch the sign in the window to an "author signing today" poster.

This might sound like overkill, but I like to present bookstore managers with a token gift for being kind enough to let me sign in their store. I've had coffee mugs printed with a Hannibal Jones logo. I present one to the manager as a thank-you for inviting me. I've been surprised at the big reaction I often get to this small gift, and I'm pretty sure these managers remember me when I see them again.

In addition to the items I've already listed for signings, you might consider putting out a small bowl of candy. It gives people who don't want to get close a reason to stop by your table. A guest book is also a good idea. While you sign books, customers can add their name and e-mail address to your ledger. That way you can contact them with special offers and add them to your newsletter mailing list. Be sure to bring two pens that you really like. You want to sign those books with style. Once I found my favorite pen, I bought a handful and always have them with me.

No book signing is going to make or break you as an author, so feel free to experiment with your approach. When I started, I preferred to sit at my display table but as time has passed I've become more comfortable standing most of the time. I say hello to everyone who passes my table. If I catch their eye, even for a second, I invite them to help themselves to a brochure or bookmark. I might mention that I'm the author that sign is talking about, or simply ask if they read mysteries. Another ice breaker that works for me is to say, "Welcome to my book signing" as people approach. My objective is to engage each person in conversation, at least long enough to find out if he might enjoy my book.

You might prefer to be beside the door, handing your brochure to each person who enters. If traffic is slow that might get more folks' attention. Just be sure you can get to your table quickly where the books are for signing—and that the manager won't be upset that you're catching people on their way in.

If traffic is slow, move around the store. Keep one of your books with you and wander near the section where your book is on the shelf. If you come across someone browsing in your section, it's okay to start a conversation. If she turns out to be a fan of your genre, tell her that's the kind of thing you write and hand her your book. That conversation can easily lead to a sale to that person or someone else in the aisle that happens to be listening.

The Aftermath

Signings always have stated hours, but I generally stay as long as the manager will let me. The manager may not know the best time for your signing, and the hour after your scheduled ending time could be a gold mine. However, the first time the manager hints that it's time to wrap up, do so. You want this person to have only happy memories of you.

When I started out, I did a lot of consignment signings, bringing the books with me. I learned that small bookstores will usually pay you on the spot while larger ones will want to send you a check. It doesn't matter, but while you're in the store you should come to agreement about how many of your books sold. During that conversation is the time to tell the manager you'd like to leave a few copies behind on the shelves and that you'd be happy to sign them for her. Be sure you have your "Author Autographed Copy" stickers handy in case the manager doesn't have any. Again, place the books on the shelf yourself in the proper section, front facing out.

Once you get bookstores to start ordering books from a distributor for your signings, things change. After two or three orders, the warehouse will have more than two or three copies of your book in stock. The more the manager sees there, the more likely he is to order instead of asking you to bring the books with you. The more that happens, the more the warehouse stocks. Those numbers say "successful signings" to a bookstore manager and make it easier for her to say yes to you. But even that good news can have a bad side.

Sometimes managers order more books than you can sign at an event. If those books hang around the store too long, they get returned to the distributor for credit. If you're self-published, that means the distributor sends the books back to you, at your expense. POD authors will end up paying shipping and handling charges that add up quickly. If you're with a small press, your publisher will be quick to tell you that returns cut deeply into its already paper-thin profit margin. In all cases, returns may arrive too damaged to sell.

There are things you can do to reduce returns. Before you leave, tell the manager that you had a lot of fun and ask her if she'd like to do this again. If the answer is yes, schedule another signing right then. That prompts the store to hold onto your books until you return to sign and sell the rest of them.

Once you have discussed the future signing, clean up your area, gather all your posters and sales material, and get out of the manager's way.

That's nearly the end of your book signing, but it isn't really over until you get home and send that handwritten thank-you note to the person in charge of coordinating your event. May I suggest you use one of those book cover postcards?

The Double Variation

Unless your ego has gotten out of control, you might want to try a team signing. I've shared several signings with K. S. Brooks, author of *Lust for Danger*. She has a big personality, and between us we are able to turn a signing into an event. Since we both send out news releases, hand out bookmarks, and greet people in the store, the signings we do together get double marketing. Store managers understand that two writers are more exciting than one, so they are more likely to say yes to scheduling an event. If this sounds like a fun idea to you, make sure you choose an author you like and whose work you like. People will ask you each if the other's book is any good, and you'd better not hesitate when you answer.

If you have multiple writing friends, consider offering a large store a panel of authors to sign all afternoon or evening. When I was published by a POD company I did this twice at Barnes and Noble stores (where I was told it was against company policy to handle POD books), and both times were great successes. One was enough of an event for C-SPAN2's Book TV to turn up with a camera. We had something for everyone, so if a browser said, "that's not my kind of thing," we just passed him down the line.

I was fortunate to find these opportunities at bookstores that had been approached by several other authors. In those cases, the managers assembled the panel of writers. But as a member of a writer's club or association gathering a group of like-minded authors isn't hard.

Others do this bigger and better than I ever could. Consider "The Outfit," a collective of eleven of the biggest and best Chicago crime writers including Sean Chercover, Barbara D'Amato, Libby Hellmann and Marcus Sakey. They blog together (theoutfitcollective.blogspot.com), make appearances together, and actively promote each other's' work. I've got to believe they draw a crowd anytime four or more of them are in the same bookstore or library.

16. Books in Nonbookstores

A lot of books are sold in this country in stores that are not dedicated to literature. I haven't had any luck getting my local supermarket to add my novels to its shelves yet, but here are a few other options that have worked for me and/or author friends of mine.

Card and Gift Stores

These shops, usually hidden in malls or shopping centers, carry lots of books but rarely offer fiction. However, one friend of mine has done well placing her romance novels in them. Her book covers are very Harlequinesque, and she has a small display near the bridal gifts section, a part of the store rarely visited by men. The books move steadily, and she sets up occasional signings.

Beauty parlors

I'm told this is another prime spot for books oriented to a female audience. I suppose it is a place where people do a lot of sitting and waiting, so it makes sense that they want a good read. I haven't tried setting up my mysteries in my barbershop yet, but who knows?

Airport shops

Okay, these places are really more newsstand than bookstore, but people do show up at them looking for something to read, and fiction is almost always their choice. Your "local author" sticker adds to the value of your book here. Now, not only is it the perfect in-flight read, it's also a memento of your city for them to take home for themselves or as a gift.

You should also ask about putting your books on their shelves on a consignment basis. Your "local author, local setting" stickers are powerful sales tools here. Visit the store often to replenish the stock, and offer to do signings on a regular basis. Remember, this is the only store you go to that does not rely on repeat business. If you signed there once a month for a year, it would be unusual for you to see the same customer's face twice. Meanwhile, you're spreading your novels all over the world.

If your books are handled by a distributor, don't overlook the bookstores in airports. There are three airports within an hour's drive of my house, and until Borders when out of business they held a total of six stores. I signed successfully at four of them and was invited back several times.

Specialty Outlets

When you go shopping, keep one eye open for a store that fits the theme of your novel. If you see a connection, the store manager might too. For example, there is a shop in the mall nearest me that sells nothing but fantasy game gear. Teens and young adults gather there to play fantasy games all day on the weekends. Surely, if I had written a book with a sword, an elf, or a Pegasus on the cover, I could convince this place to display a few copies.

Several places in my area feature live, interactive mysteries. These are generally allied with a dinner theater or hotel. If you write mysteries with a little humor in them, you might want to approach these places to add to their revenue by selling your books or to roll your novel into the price of their performance and offer them as a premium with each ticket.

Anyone who has a cash register can sell your books, and it never hurts to ask about a book signing. I haven't given up on my local supermarket.

Austin S. Camacho

ADVANCED
TECHNIQUES

"If you're coasting, you're going downhill."

17. Advertising

Up to this point, this book has been strictly do-it-yourself. That has been my approach in real life, although I realize that it's not everyone's cup of java. In this chapter, we'll discuss some of the things you can do that require some serious investment, but also may offer a serious payoff.

Mailing to the Masses

You can search the Internet and for less than a hundred dollars find software that will enable you to send bulk e-mail to the millions of online households in this country. It's the cyber equivalent of the junk mail you find in your mailbox every day. This is a very popular form of marketing today, but I don't know if that approach would net you any sales. I am quite certain, however, that the lost good will could not possibly be worth whatever money you earned. Just think how angry you are about the junk mail that slithers into your own e-mail inbox every day.

If you really want to try a mass e-mail campaign, consider using one of the larger companies such as postmasterdirect.com. They use only "opt-in" e-mail addresses. Are these really the addresses of people who have asked for junk mail? Well, sort of. Try to remember the last time you entered a contest or accepted a free gift online. You may have filled out a form of demographic information. Near the bottom there was a box, already checked, that said something like "send me valuable update on this subject." Didn't bother to uncheck the box? Then you just opted in. Or was there a page of the form that was a list of possible interests for you to check off? You just asked for e-mail selling you books, records, or whatever you checked as your interests. Does that mean you really want all this e-mail?

And, by the way, while these e-mails are very inexpensive on a per-person basis, you may be daunted by postmasterdirect's minimum order size of a thousand dollars.

On the other hand, people react much less violently to the junk mail that pours into their physical mailboxes each day, especially if it is fairly and honestly labeled, is addressed to them (as opposed to "occupant"), and politely offers them something they might conceivably want. There are several companies, also listed online, that will be happy to sell you the equivalent of mailing labels to attach to your outgoing e-mail advertising. However, there's a limit to the degree to which you can fine-tune those lists. Everyone is happy to give you a certain geographic area, but I had to make an exhaustive search to find a company who could sell me a list of mystery readers (5-starlists.com).

If you can't find the targeted list you need, consider going back to that list of magazines you built at the very beginning of this book. If you didn't make such a list, well, I'm not talking to you anymore. But assuming you did, you have a valuable resource at hand. You can bet that the same people who might want to read your western short stories will want to know about your western novel. So call the circulation department at *American Western Magazine* and ask if the publication rents its mailing list to appropriate advertisers.

To raise awareness of the Maryland Writers Association's annual conference, I contacted *Writer's Digest* and arranged to mail to their subscribers in Maryland; Washington, D.C.; and northern Virginia. About twelve hundred names cost us around four hundred dollars, but we knew we were talking to the people who might want to sign up for our conference. And in fact, we saw a number of new faces there who, I'm sure, were responding to our mailing.

In a similar way, the readers of *Eye Spy* won't be offended if they get something in the mail about your new espionage thriller. Be careful, though. The mailing list of *Spy* couldn't care less about your book. Their interest is true fact espionage, not fiction.

I do not recommend mailing anything to a stranger that calls for him to open an envelope. Tossing your piece is so much easier! And I believe the days of the return envelope have passed unless you are selling something someone really needs, and no matter how badly we wish it were otherwise, no one really needs a new novel or short story collection. Instead, send all the reasons why the recipient would want your book and list all the ways he can get your book. List your Web site, your publisher's Web site if sales are possible there, the local bookstores that stock your books, and Amazon.com and BN.com. If your mailing piece is sufficiently convincing, a certain number of people will be moved to get to their computers and make that purchase.

The Postcard Story

Those postcards you ordered not long after you made that magazine list (right?) are the perfect tool for mailings. You can use them to announce your book to potential buyers or as reminders later on. As with any promotional effort, timing is critical. Rather than bore you with another story of my own writing life as proof, I'll let Penny Sansevieri tell you about her first direct mail success:

"I began using postcards when I was promoting my first book, "*The Cliffhanger*," and I've used them for every book since. I always print my book cover on the front. Typically, I'll get 500 printed with my book announcement for an initial mailing and another 500 with a blank back that I can use as reminders or thank you cards. By seeing my book cover repeatedly, people will remember it--and, hopefully, remember me too.

And you're not limited to announcements and thank you notes! Blank postcards can be used for just about anything. For example, the 2000 presidential election took place while I was marketing "*The Cliffhanger.*" All through the ups and downs of counting chads (both dimpled and nondimpled) they kept referring to this election as a "'cliffhanger.'" I sent out 500 postcards with this message:

> *Getting tired of the presidential cliffhanger?*
> *Try this one.*
> The Cliffhanger, *a novel.*
> *No politics involved.*

Did I have these postcards printed especially for this? No way! Knowing that the election could get called at any moment, I was frantic to get these out. So, I purchased clear labels at my local office supply store and printed them on my little inkjet printer, adhered them to the postcards and sent them off. A local TV anchor loved the tie-in, held up and read my postcard and told everyone watching to go out and buy my book. "*The Cliffhanger*" shot up to the #1 best-selling book in San Diego where it remained for three months.

It only took one mention. And those who didn't respond were at least reminded of my book again.

Repetition is important. If someone you've been pitching sees your book enough, they'll think it's probably worth a call back.

The key is consistency."

If a coming holiday or a present news event ties in to your book, seize the opportunity as Penny did. She confirms that she also uses her postcards as thank-you cards, and even to announce that a media kit is on its way to television, radio, and newspaper people.

PMA Mailing: A Good Idea That Didn't Work

Some writers have told me that the most effective form of direct mail marketing can be achieved through membership in an industry organization called the IBPA, the Independent Book Publishers Association.

Membership in IBPA is not a casual expense. Publishers pay based on the number of employees, but for individual authors the cost is $185 per year. Oddly, if you self-publish – that is, you are a publishing company of one – your annual cost is $129. Either way, you need to sell a few books to cover that, so if you're like me, you need to believe you're going to recoup that investment from what the association has to offer you. It has several direct mailing programs that might just do that. For a fee, your book can be included in full-color mailings to librarians, reviewers, bookstores, and individuals.

For example, IBPA will send your promotional flyer along with those of other members to acquisition librarians throughout the country. We're talking public libraries, corporate libraries, and school and university libraries. The mailings go out every other month and costs $215. Only you can know if you'll make enough sales to cover that, but it might be worth a try.

IBPA also sends a quarterly color catalog that is more like a newsletter to approximately 3,000 book reviewers at newspapers, magazines, websites, blogs, radio and television shows. Bounce-back cards are included in this mailing for reviewer to request specific titles. Inclusion costs $210. This can pay off if you list your book three or four months before its "release date."

A very similar newsletter-type color catalog is mailed to approximately thirty-five hundred booksellers every other month for $230 a shot. I'm less enthusiastic about this one if your books are still nonreturnable.

Most interesting to me was the Target Marketing Mailing, which presents your novel to specific booksellers, librarians, and reviewers based on your genre. The fiction catalogs go out three times a year. In this case, you pay $350 to avoid being surrounded by religious subjects, cookbooks, and self-help titles. This seemed like a no-brainer.

But I have to follow the evidence. Inclusion in a bookstore mailing brought me nothing. Really, not one response. A mailing to reviewers brought requests for a dozen review copies. I was filled with optimism as I mailed out those books, but a year later not one of those reviews had surfaced. I can only assume that people at twelve different newspapers across the country added a free mystery novel to their bookshelves.

Just because I didn't gain anything from this idea doesn't mean it couldn't work for you. But be aware that if you decide to try this type of mailing, you are putting money at risk and stepping outside of my evidence-based marketing concept.

This is not to say that membership in the PMA can't help your marketing. In fact, the group offers one other bit of help that could be most important to a POD novelist. The PMA trade distribution acceptance program looks at titles from members that have not yet been stocked by the major bookstore chains. If you submit a book and it's accepted, Independent Publishers Group will act as a distributor for the title as long as Borders or Barnes & Noble has never stocked it. You can have a wholesale relationship with Ingram or Baker & Taylor and still be eligible for this program as long as you own the title's ISBN.

18. Making the Most of the Media

It doesn't take any special talent to be impressive when you do a radio interview or when the local newspaper reporter approaches you at your book signing. In fact, after teaching media training to Department of Defense officials for a couple of decades, I can tell you the basics of what you need to know in three short sentences: Smile. Be prepared. Know your messages.

Smile and the World Smiles with You

When you find yourself in a radio studio, you might think you are isolated from the world. But you will notice that the host is working very hard to get you to relax and to establish a relationship with you in the few seconds before the mike goes hot. That's because he knows that your personality will reach right through those wires and, believe it or not, unless you're a government official, the host wants the people on the other end of the radio to like you.

Don't make the amateur mistake of thinking smiles only count when a camera is rolling. Contrary to popular belief, people can hear your smile right through their radios. The same is true to a surprising extent when a journalist paints your portrait in print in a local newspaper or magazine. Believe me, if you radiate enthusiasm and joy it will find its way into the story.

Remember, you are not in that interview to talk about a scholarly journal or educational textbook. You are a storyteller. People will want to read your stories only if they are entertaining. And let's face it, if your book doesn't make you happy, if it doesn't get you excited, you can't expect others to get excited enough to want to spend an evening with it.

Boy Scout Writer

Boy Scouts aren't the only people who need to be prepared. You should never travel without all the supplies you need, and for interviews, your supplies are information. The best way to make sure you're ready for whatever comes at you during an interview is to make a list of the most common questions writers get asked. You know them. If you don't, just think back to the last few time you told someone you were an author. I'll bet they asked you things such as: What's your book about? Why did you write it? How long did it take you? What's the theme? When is the next one coming out? Once you've got your own top ten questions, write out the answers.

Now comes the hard part. Practice! Say your answers over and over until they come easily. Roleplay a little bit, and record yourself. By listening to the recording you can make sure that you sound like you're smiling and that your answers aren't too long. If it takes more than twenty-five seconds to explain what your book is about, shorten the answer! No one wants a sound bite or quote that long. Keep at it until you can roll out your responses without a lot of stumbling. You should be ready to talk about your book in a minute, in five to ten minutes, and in ten to thirty minutes, so that you can fit whatever time slot is booked.

You should also have some anecdotes in your kit. Insightful writing pro and literary agent Chip MacGregor (ChipMacGregor.com) says that there are only two kinds of interviewers: those who have not read your book and those who don't know how to read. Never assume the interviewer has read your book. MacGregor also warns that it's much harder to prepare for the unknown, so unless you've done a lot of this before, don't agree to take caller questions on the air. This only leads to random nut jobs, lonely widows, and hyperventilating outraged types, with the occasional know-it-all blowhard who loves the sound of his own voice.

Your first interview won't be all you want it to be. Be sure to ask the TV or radio interviewer for a copy of your interview so you can study your performance, and record any questions for which you didn't have an immediate answer. Soon you'll have a response for anything you might get asked.

The Media Loves the Message

As I tell my government clients, there is no mystery to giving a good interview as long as you stick to the truth and stay pleasant. If I do offer anything that might be called a trick in my media training, it is the importance of knowing your messages. You should have three messages for your book. Why? Because people like things that come in threes. It's a comfortable number to remember, for them and for you. Just figure out the most important things you want people to remember about your book, after the title and author's name of course. As an example here are my own three messages for my first novel, *Blood and Bone*:

1. Anyone who loves a good mystery will enjoy this book, and you'll never guess the ending.

2. I'm a local author, and my book is set locally. So you can read about places you know and support the local writing community.

3. Today you can own a signed collector's edition of my novel. John Grisham is more famous, but he's not here right now to sign his.

You're welcome to adapt my messages, or yours might be entirely different. Maybe your science fiction novel has a message about the future you want to spread. Perhaps the historical accuracy of your western is an important point. Use whatever makes sense, as long as you know what your messages are.

Now that you have your messages, what will you do with them? Well, that's the real trick. You see, your three messages are the answer to every question you get. I don't mean that you should avoid direct answers. But no matter what you are asked, you should attach some form of one of your messages to every answer you give. This may take a bit of practice, but once you're in the habit it won't be hard at all. For example:

Q: What's your book about?

A: It revolves around a child dying of leukemia and my detective's pursuit of his long-lost father, the last hope for the boy's needed bone marrow transplant. His search draws him into a mystery with so many twists that you'll never guess the ending.

Q: How long did it take you?

A: More than a year. Some of it I thought up right here in this cafe/library/bookstore. It's full of local settings so you can read about places you know.

Get the idea? Give it a try. If you know your messages, if you're prepared for questions, and if you remember to smile, you'll be an author who TV and radio hosts and newspaper writers want to talk to again and again.

Your Comfort Zone

If you're really advanced, you may be sending your news releases out to get interviews. But in my experience, you have to have a pretty special piece of fiction to get onto a television news or talk show. It's hard to find the news hook that makes a novelist a draw. That doesn't mean don't look for one. For example, if you write fantasy and happen to be a J. R. R. Tolkien expert, you could probably have gotten yourself on the air the week before *The Two Towers* was released. Similarly, the spy novelist who was a huge James Bond aficionado could probably get on to comment on the fiftieth anniversary film and just mention his own book at the beginning and end of the segments. And if your thriller that came out last year related to antiterrorist activity and the threat Hamas poses to Israel, your research probably qualified you to speak on local TV or radio.

More likely, though, your interviews will come because someone has unfilled space on a show or in the newspaper, and you happen to be speaking or signing publicly. The news hook is simply that you are a local author with a new book out. And the reporter wants to get a sound bite or two out of you and get on with his life. Just remember that he needs you right then as much as you need him, so don't let him run the interview. If it's not a good time for you, say so.

I can imagine how difficult this would be. You're doing a book signing or reading and suddenly someone's taking your picture or asking you in-depth questions about how this romance novel you've written relates to your own love life. Is this your one big chance to be in the paper?

Well, no. This is your one big chance to sign books. It's okay to politely tell the reporter that you'll be happy to talk to him over a cup of coffee fifteen minutes after your signing is over, or right after everyone who just heard you read has asked their questions and taken away whatever books they may want. You're here for your adoring public, but as soon as you have done your duty, you'll give that reporter your undivided attention.

It's even easier for radio, because whether a reporter is pursuing you with a portable recorder or you got his interest by sending a release and following it with a phone call, it's better for everyone if you're relaxed when you speak. Ask to do the interview from home, on the telephone. That way you're literally at home, in your jammies and fuzzy slippers maybe, but with all your notes and promotional material spread out in front of you.

Working in your comfort zone will allow you to give your best possible interview, and the better the interview, the better your chances of being asked to do it again and again.

19. Outsourcing— Hiring a Publicist

Some may think that this should be the first step, but I consider it the last. I understand the attraction of hiring a professional to do all the work I've described in the last hundred pages, but even if you have the resources, I recommend doing it yourself for a while first. That's the only way you'll ever be able to judge if the person you're paying is really any better qualified than you are to promote your book. Once you have a feel for what you think should happen, you may decide that you simply don't have time to do what you think should be done. Or maybe you're out of ideas and want to bring some fresh thinking into the process. At that point, it may be time to hire a publicist to help you out.

How Do You Choose?

There are a lot of professional publicists out there, but unlike doctors, lawyers, and other professionals, there is no association to help you choose the greats from the pretenders. Also, like any other profession, there are specialists in every aspect. To me, the most important thing to look for in a publicist is book-marketing experience. Book promotion bears little resemblance to running a political campaign or marketing toothpaste. It is perfectly reasonable to ask for references, and to speak with them. At this point, you don't need to know how happy the other author was with the publicist's personality or how supportive he was. Your question is plain and simple—what did this publicist do for your sales? Clients should be able to give you specific metrics like how many radio interviews they've done or how many book signings the publicist booked.

What will it cost?

This is another area where being shy will not pay. We are all reluctant to ask about charges when hiring a professional, be it a doctor, lawyer, or accountant. But those people have fairly standard rates whereas the charges for publicity or promotion are all over the map. You may be comfortable with an hourly fee. That way, your cost is related to the amount of effort the publicist puts into your campaign. Or you may be more like me and prefer to pay a predictable amount for a particular service. Even beyond that choice, there are variables. After you pay for the media packets, do you also pay for the postage? When she's calling the media, is the cost of the phone calls extra?

When you ask about pricing, one clue to professionalism will be if the publicist starts asking you questions. What cities do you want covered? How much time do you want to spend on the road or on the radio or at signings? How much are you willing to do for yourself? This is when you begin to see how the relationship with this person will go.

Most importantly, make sure the publicist really engages with you. Expect a lot of talking. In fact, you want this person to get excited about your book. You'll need to be comfortable with this person and establish a relationship that allows for a free-wheeling exchange of ideas. If your book is published through a print-on-demand company, chat enough to get convinced that he knows what a POD book is and understands the limitations you face. If you're self-published be sure she has worked with self-published authors before. Remember, your successful promotional plan won't look much like what the major publishers do.

Don't assume that a quiet demeanor must mean that the publicist is a deep thinker or some sort of genius. Yes, very often still waters do run deep. But sometimes, still waters are just stagnant.

Now That I've Got One, What Do I Want Her to Do?

While I am not a big fan of one-shot promotions, I also don't recommend you begin your work with a publicist with a huge national campaign. Your publicist should offer a la carte options. Choose something fairly small and inexpensive and see how your publicist handles the sample assignment.

For example, if she suggests a media blitz with a new news release, don't just evaluate the quality of the release. Ask how she will prequalify targets. This is by far the harder part of the job and will tell you if this publicist has the one thing you don't have— connections. Find out who she knows at these places, and what kind of follow-up is included in the plan. If she's launching your release to a blind list, the plan won't be very effective. And without follow-up, she will never know who not to send to in the future. I used to work in a government office that produced a quarterly magazine for service members and veterans. Our magazine didn't take advertising or do reviews, but that didn't stop faxes from rolling off our machine almost every day with news releases for new books. Every time that happened, somebody was wasting some author's money.

If prices vary among publicists you like, ask about guarantees. One may promise to approach a certain number of radio stations, for example. But if the other guarantees you a minimum number of on-air interviews, that person is worth a higher fee. If you're asking the publicist to design products for you (brochures, postcards, bookmarks) ask to see examples of past work and ask yourself honestly if it looks professional and eye catching.

If your test assignment is a big success, you may eventually want to move up to a full-force program. This could be a six-month plan starting before your next book's release. Even then, I recommend that you think long and hard before launching a national campaign or tour, especially for POD authors. If your books are not returnable, that is a difficult objection to overcome with an out-of-town bookstore, and you surely don't want to haul hundreds of books across country. Even if your books are returnable, small numbers in the nearest warehouse will make bookstore managers very reluctant to have you sign for them. It may be best to keep your media blitz and publicity attack inside the area you're willing to drive for signings, readings and in-person interviews. When your distributor's nearest warehouse starts stocking you, you might then want to try moving your activity into a neighboring area.

A good publicist can be your partner in the fight to take your book to new heights, but you'll only find the right fit if you take the time to speak with a few. Don't settle on a publicist until you meet the person with whom you can work smoothly.

20. Insourcing: A Little Help from Your Friends

The chapter title may sound as if I'm going to tell you to send your friends out to sell your books. That's not quite what I have in mind, but the result can be similar. The point is that your family and friends often want to help you to succeed. It can help you a lot to tell them just how they can be most helpful. Here are a few ideas.

Force Multiplier

If you have friends who really want to help your book grow, they can become part of your success. Assemble your informal promotional team and let them know how you promote your writing and ask them to imitate you. The key here is that they know people you don't know. Do you talk about your book to almost everyone you meet? Ask your special team to do the same. Give them postcards and postage, and ask them to send the postcards to people they think might be interested in what you write. A personal note from them is more likely to get the attention of their friends than a note from you ever will.

Do you e-mail out a newsletter? They can help you by forwarding your newsletter to others with a brief recommendation to read what they find to be a very interesting journal of one author's progress. Likewise, they can send e-mails to alert their friends and family to every bit of you that is accessible by computer— your site, your video trailer, and anything else you've done.

Bookstore Presence

Most of your good friends are probably readers. Each of them probably visits a favorite bookstore on a regular basis. It would be easy for each of them to make friends with the store manager over time, especially if they buy books on most of their visits. And if each of your good friends asks the manager in four or five bookstores to order a few copies of your book, well, you do the math.

Your friends also can let the manager know that they know an author who would love to hold a book signing event at their store. Once your books are in a bookstore, your friends can make sure they stay on the shelves with the cover facing out, and remind the manager to order more when the supply gets dangerously low.

And, by the way, the same friends, being readers, can put a bug into the ear of the right people at the local library.

Event advance team

Some of the ways friends can help before an author event are pretty subtle. Signs and brochures in a bookstore before your signing are valuable, but their importance can be magnified by one or two people just standing around in the store talking about your books. Other customers will overhear their chatter and that alone can kick off a little bit of buzz. And buzz is good.

Your pals can also keep an eye on brochures in the store, refilling if they run out.

Packing the House

When you give a reading or signing anywhere, people will judge your success by two parameters. Only you and the store manager will know for sure how many copies you sold at a particular event, but everyone present will know how many people turned out to see you.

In this case, your team can serve two purposes. One, of course, is to be there. They should turn up separately and stay as long as possible. The more faces in the place, the more your reading or signing will seem like an event. It wouldn't hurt for them to mention to someone else there how much they enjoyed your book.

Team members can also help by modeling desired behavior for other crowd members. At a signing that can mean little more than walking up and talking to you, being friendly, and picking up a book to read the back cover and check out any reviews you have printed inside. You want people to handle the merchandise, and seeing someone do that helps others to know it's okay. At a signing, team members will be quiet when people are supposed to be listening, laugh when you make a joke, and applaud at the appropriate time. You would be amazed how much easier that can make a reading event.

Follow-up Feedback

As I said before, when you give a radio interview or do a reading, you're giving a performance. But is it a good performance? That's hard for you to judge when you're doing it. But a good friend can watch and listen more objectively and even take notes to give you a clear report of how well you held people's attention, expressed your messages, remembered to smile, and all the other important things you need to do during public appearances. This kind of feedback can be invaluable in refining your presentation.

The same kind of outside observation can be useful even during a book signing. A friend who is supportive can tell you what you're saying (or not saying) that is causing store visitors to walk on by instead of stopping to talk. What are you doing that makes people want to stop at your table? If you knew, you'd do more of it, right? A friend can tell you, but only if you ask.

They're Special: Show That You Know It

If you do have a team of supportive friends, make sure you reward their support. In my experience, this calls for two important tactics.

First, they deserve special gifts. You know those coffee mugs you give to bookstore managers? Your supportive friends deserve them too. But they should also have something that is unique to them. How about giving each of them a t-shirt or a baseball cap with your insignia or book cover on it? This kind of a gift does triple duty. It makes your friends feel special. And if they're making an effort to support your writing career, they are. It also gives your supporters the feeling of being part of a team. They should all know each other, and when you give someone their shirt, cap or whatever, you should inform the whole crew so they can welcome the new member. They should be a small, very exclusive fraternity.

On a more selfish note, this kind of gift promotes your work. Someone walking around in a shirt or hat displaying your symbol or book cover is like putting up a billboard or a magnetic sign on your car. It increases the public's awareness of your name and work. If several of these people live in the same area, they will begin to look like the seeds of a movement. In fact, they may be just that.

The second tactic may be even more important. Your most supportive friends deserve special information. You want them to feel as if they are part of your success, so keep them in the loop. Let them know where you are with the next manuscript. Make sure they are first to know where you'll appear or what your next project is. Let them read early versions of your stories. This last bit can pay off twice, since they can be enlisted as early readers, editors, and proofreaders.

I haven't reached this point yet myself, but you could set up a special part of your Web site, accessible only with a password that only special friends get. That would be a place to put character sketches and manuscripts long before anyone else can see them. You might even solicit fan fiction about your characters and post their writing there. Anything that keeps your support team involved in your writing is to your advantage. The more they feel they are part of your march to best-seller status, the more they want to help you.

21. Thinking outside the Box

To sell nonfiction or how-to books, you need to convince people that you have knowledge that they need to share. To market fiction, you really only need to get people's attention so that they will examine your book. After that, the book makes the sale. I'm sure there are a few hundred ways to get people's attention that I haven't thought of, so I encourage you to open up that same imagination that created a fictional universe between two covers and look for new and different ways to promote your fiction. There is so much that hasn't been done.

Sign Differently

How about a marathon signing? Your newsletter hook could be that a local author will meet every person who walks into a particular bookstore or other venue all day. Stay there the entire time the place is open, set up and ready to sign. Have lunch in the store. Make it a writer's endurance test.

How about taking your laptop in for a demonstration? Sit in the front window of your favorite venue and invite people to watch you create. Jewelry makers do this all the time at craft fairs. Make a poster of your outline, and let passers-by know where you are in the story and what plot point you're working on. Maybe you can get others to be engaged in creating your next novel.

Read Differently

How about gathering a team of writers to appear together at signings? A team of four mystery writers travels under the name "Nuns, Mothers and Others" and never has a problem getting reading gigs. Their books are similar and draw the same audience, but four authors get a lot more publicity than one can. You could go a step further and all dress the same, or find three or four writers whose characters have something significant in common to make your reading an attractive package.

How about staging a read-off, or "battle of the authors" where each writer gets to read for a certain amount of time and the audience gets to pick a winner? This might inspire the authors to give more spirited performances of their work, bring props, and so forth.

How about gathering a cast of friends and performing scenes from your book? Or turning part of

195

your book into a role-playing game like those mystery parties that some groups do?

Publish Differently

How about printing one chapter of your novel as a pamphlet to give away? As a takeaway piece, it could bring you additional sales after a personal appearance. Or, stacked up at the cash register of your favorite bookstore it could be a goodwill builder for them and an awareness raiser for you. And what if you got a chapter inserted in the local newspaper or as a giveaway paper in your area?

How about starting a small magazine and filling it with your own stories and stories written by other local authors? As a group you could split the cost and get some valuable publicity for everyone involved.

If that expense frightens you, maybe you'd like to start an e-zine instead. These electronic magazines are very popular with the computer-savvy, and you can create the entire thing in the comfort of your own home. Offer your writing friends links to their Web sites in exchange for stories and articles, and you'll end up with more content than you know what to do with.

How about using the POD process to publish a mosaic novel? You start a story and pass it to another local author to write the next section. When you're finished, you have the ten or twelve authors split the publishing cost and you can all sell the book, which promotes you all. If even one of you becomes a "big name," it promotes everyone's status.

Present Yourself Differently

How about starting a television or radio show on your local public access station? It will require a certain amount of time, but it will also put your face and name in front of the public on a regular basis. You could start a talk show and have local authors, bookstore owners, magazine editors, and other related people as your guests. You might never mention your own book except in conversation, but you might become the best-known author in your area. Even bookstores that don't like POD or self-published books might be embarrassed not to have yours on their shelves.

How about arranging a signing event in someone's home? You could offer refreshments, do a reading, and find (or create) some entertaining games that relate to your genre. Make sure you have the soundtrack from appropriate movies. Consider giving prizes to people who show up in costume.

How about writing a nonfiction book? Has your research qualified you to write the story of a particular Native American tribe, a catalog of the hundred greatest fictional spies, or a book on how to put more romance into a relationship? Declare yourself an expert and go for it. Hey, why do you think I wrote this book? Sure, I want to help my fellow self-published, POD and small press novelists reach success, but I also hope it will help me to promote *Blood and Bone, Collateral Damage, The Troubleshooter, Damaged Goods* and future novels in the Hannibal Jones series.

Now, it's your turn to do some brainstorming. Go out and try something new and different, and let me know how you did. If your unique idea is a success, I'll want to feature it in the next edition of *Successfully Marketing Your Fiction in the 21st Century*.

22. Final Words

I started this book with three basic principles. I want to end it with three bits of advice.

Keep Trying

The harder I work at marketing my books, the luckier I get. Unless you decide that your book needs improving, never give up on marketing it. You need to build momentum to get your title recognized.

Don't expect everything you try to be a huge success. Learn the lesson from each failure and apply evidence-based marketing, but don't stop. In this way, marketing is much like skiing. If you're not falling, you're not trying.

Keep Learning

I've included a list of my favorite marketing manuals at the back of the book. Read them closely and evaluate with a cool head which ideas they offer are appropriate for you. Pay special attention to what has not worked for others so you can avoid some of the pitfalls. Learn from the mistakes of others. You won't live long enough to make them all yourself.

Be Realistic

Rare indeed is the author who hits one out of the park on his first swing, and some of today's best-known names never had a legitimate best seller until they gathered an audience with a dozen smaller books. By the same token, don't be shaken by that event at which you only sign one book or by the reviewer who says you could make more money as a butcher. We're novelists. By definition we are chasing rainbows. Just remember that if you want the rainbow, you've got to put up with the rain.

<u>Shout Outs</u>

I just want to point out a few of the folks who have really helped my promotional efforts over the years.

Melanie Rigney—A past editor of *Writer's Digest* magazine and editorial director of Writer's Digest Books, Melanie has helped hundreds of authors, publishers, and literary agents with manuscript evaluations, book proposals, content editing, copy editing, and coaching. I am blessed to have her as my friend and as the editor who consistently helps me improve my work. Find an editor like her, and you can be confident that success will find you. (www.editorforyou.com)

Gary Amoth—Owner of the Hard Bean Coffee and Bookseller in Annapolis, Maryland, Gary has been encouraging to local authors and always is willing to stock my books or surrender some space for a signing. (www.beansandbooks.com/default.htm)

Nora Partlow and Scott Mitchell—The owners of St. Elmo's Coffee Pub in Alexandria, Virginia, were the first people to open their doors to me, allowing me to do my first-ever reading in a warm and welcoming atmosphere. (www.stelmoscoffeepub.com)

Shelley Glodowsky—The lady at Midwest Book Review who gave *Blood and Bone* a five star review, my first real review, which has helped sell a lot of books. (www.midwestbookreview.com)

Warren Murphy—Two-time Edgar Award winner and creator of The Destroyer adventure series, Warren was the first big-name author who was kind enough to read my novels and give me a blurb as well as much encouragement. He is not just a writer, but a gentleman as well. (www.warrenmurphy.com)

Libby Fisher Hellman—Once you publish four award-winning novels and have been president of Sisters in Crime, you don't need to give your valuable time to upstart newbies, but Libby was kind enough to read and write a blurb for my latest manuscript so publishers might more likely look at it. She's a very special lady in a tough, competitive business. (www.hellmann.com/mystery-author/index.html).

Cynthia Lauth—Her enthusiasm for my work has made managers say yes to signings in their stores, twenty-five times in the first year. More than a friend, fan, and support, Cyndi has done more than anyone to help me get my books into the hands of eager readers.

Sharon Lucas – President of The Reading Divas – www.thereadingdivas.com – Sharon is a leader in the book club community and very supportive to authors big and small. She has welcomed me to meetings of her book club, prompted other books clubs to host me, and created events than any author would want to be part of.

Resources:

Marketing Books:

1,001 Ways to Market Your Books—John Kremer

Complete Guide to Book Marketing—David Cole

The Complete Guide to Book Publicity—Jodee Blanco

The Complete Guide to Self-Publishing: Everything You Need to Know to Write, Publish, Promote and Sell Your Own Book—Tom Ross and Marilyn Ross

Guerrilla Marketing for Writers: 100 Weapons to Help You Sell Your Work—Jay Conrad Levinson, Rick Frishman, and Michael Larsen

Jump Start Your Book Sales: A Money-Making Guide for Authors, Independent Publishers and Small Presses—Marilyn and Tom Ross

Plug Your Book! Online Book Marketing for Authors, Book Publicity through Social Networking—Steve Weber

The Self-Publishing Manual, How to Write, Print & Sell Your Own Book—Dan Poynter

Successfully Marketing Your Novel

Small Presses—Marilyn and Tom Ross

Writing the Breakout Novel by Donald Maas

The Plot Thickens: 8 Ways to Bring Fiction to Life by Noah Lukeman

The 38 Most Common Fiction Writing Mistakes: (And How to Avoid Them) by Jack M. Bickham

Self-Editing for Fiction Writers by Renni Browne and Dave King

Write Away by Elizabeth George

Techniques of the Selling Writer by Dwight V. Swain

Sample Marketing Plan

Complete manuscript, release date minus 180 days
Investigate books at bookstores for format and cover choices
Hire cover artist
Format book
Send manuscript to editor and proofreader
Join writing organizations
Join newsgroups/list-servs
Join chat rooms and appear there on a regular schedule
Join IBPA
Compile specialty magazine list
Compile list of authors for blurbs
Compile list of review pubs/reviewers
Compile list of book events to attend
Compile list of fairs/festivals to attend
Write articles/short stories/reviews

Send manuscript to publisher or printer, Release date minus 150 days
Establish release date
Submit articles/short stories/reviews to specialty magazines
Design/print business cards/bookmarks/brochures

Order postcards/stickers
Contact authors to request blurbs

Receive first order of books, release date minus 120 days
Write first news release
Mail review copy packages to chosen review sources
Purchase domain and build Web site
Locate Web sites with which to exchange links
Join Web rings
Begin "prerelease" mailing

Release date minus 60 days
Sign up for fairs and festivals 90 days in advance
Compile list of bookstores/reading sites/signing sites

Release date minus 30 days
Send news release announcing book's publication
Contact bookstore/reading sites to book readings/signings
Upon receiving second review, print review sheets
Contact media for interviews

Release date
Begin newsletter

Each month thereafter
Write & submit new news release

Submit articles/short stories/reviews to specialty magazines
Attend book events
Sign up for fairs/festivals 90 days in advance
Send appropriate PMA mailing or mail from own list
Continue to contact venues for readings/signings
Update Web site
Update review sheet
Update newsletter
Look for news hook or holiday hook for media interviews

Austin's Online Presence

My Web site: www.hannibaljonesmysteries.com

My blog ascamacho.blogspot.com/

Crimespace:
crimespace.ning.com/profile/ascamacho

Shelfari: www.shelfari.com/ascamacho

YouTube:
www.youtube.com/watch?v=Wb7AYLIauDE

Facebook: tinyurl.com/d3dzqly

LinkedIn: www.linkedin.com/myprofile?trk=tab_pro

Gather: ascamacho.gather.com

Author's Den:
www.authorsden.com/austinscamacho

CPSIA information can be obtained at www.ICGtesting.com
Printed in the USA
BVOW02s0456191213

339207BV00002B/6/P